25 YEARS · BUILT to LAST

ASHTON APPLEWHITE

A FIRESIDE BOOK

PUBLISHED BY SIMON & SCHUSTER

NEW YORK LONDON TORONTO SYDNEY TOKYO SINGAPORE

Thinking Positive

Words of Inspiration, Encouragement, and

Validation for People with AIDS and

Those Who Care for Them

FIRESIDE
Rockefeller Center
1230 Avenue of the Americas
New York, New York 10020

FIRESIDE and colophon are registered trademarks of Simon &
Schuster Inc.

Designed by Chris Welch
Manufactured in the United States of America

10   9   8   7   6   5   4   3   2   1

Library of Congress Cataloging-in-Publication Data

Applewhite, Ashton.
Thinking positive : words of inspiration, encouragement, and
validation for people with AIDS and those who care for them /
Ashton Applewhite.
p.   cm.
"A Fireside book"
1. AIDS (Disease)—Miscellanea. 2. Affirmations. 3. AIDS (Disease)—
Quotations. 4. AIDS (Disease)—Patients—Conduct of life. I. Title.
RC607.A26A68   1995
362.1'969792—dc20   94-46729
CIP

ISBN: 0-684-80266-X

The excerpt from "How to Watch Your Brother Die" is © copy-
right 1985 and 1990 by Michael Lassell. Reprinted from *Decade
Dance* (Alyson Publications, 1990) by permission of the author.

The excerpt from "Metaphor as Illness" by Charles Ortleb is
reprinted by permission of the author.

For Bob and Maria

Contents

Foreword

Thinking Positive is a collection of sayings that will help you to understand your life. The quotations are inspiring, encouraging, and validating, but they are in no way about a false sense of "thinking positive." The words contained here do not deny life's pains. They respond to them. The people quoted have all shared in the common experience—life is a labor pain. What these words help us to do is to give birth to ourselves and, therefore, make the pain worthwhile.

I always ask people if life is fair. The majority shout, "No!" I disagree. I think life is perfectly fair; after all, we are all complaining, so we must be experiencing the same thing. What we need to understand is that life is difficult, not unfair.

The words in *Thinking Positive* direct us to a new view of life, one in which adversity and afflictions can be understood and dealt with. The guilt, blame, and shame can be cast aside, and one's true worth and value can be seen. Is it easy? No! But it is a journey well worth taking. Isn't it nice to be able to look at your naked self in a mirror and think, "It's me. I'm beautiful"? This is not easy to do without confronting your own mortality and essence.

Or consider this—how would you introduce yourself to God? Again, ask yourself, What is your reason for being? It isn't only the role you play while you're here, but finding your divine essence, and taking comfort in the fact that God already knows you, so you don't need an introduction. The quotations in this book will help you to understand why you are here, and what you are here for.

AIDS and other afflictions shorten many lives, but they do not keep us from living life to the fullest in the years available to us. *Thinking Positive* will help you complete your own life, and do the one thing we were all sent here to do—love. If we do that, then we have done what we came here to do, and when the time comes for us to leave, we can leave with a satisfaction about a life that *was* complete.

We will feel grief, but it will not consume us. What our mortality teaches us is to participate in life with joy, and to contribute love in our own special way. Just as the maple leaf displays its beauty and uniqueness before letting go of the tree of life, let us be our true, unique selves and find our own path.

The dreams, images, and words that come from a deeper source than our own intellect are contained in this book. Read them and open to your own true path and inner wisdom.

Bernie S. Siegel, M.D.

Introduction

A dear friend and fellow writer, Chris Cox, died of AIDS several years ago. The program from his memorial service bore the slogan Silence = Death. The epidemic hit closer to home when my sister's husband, Bob, grew ill and died of AIDS. I watched her struggle not just with the enormity of her loss but with the stigma facing her two young daughters, which added hugely and senselessly to her burden. I rage at Bob's absence from our lives. And I rage that other friends are ailing or dead.

So many of you have lost lovers or blood relatives, or may be ill yourselves, tragedies far greater than mine. AIDS doesn't discriminate. It touches all of us: straight and gay, healthy and ill, men and women, expert and uninformed, children and adults, privileged and poor. This is why in the pages that follow I have chosen to speak of what "we" can do and of "our" needs. Suffering is not relative. No one is an expert. We all know what it is to grieve over the loss of someone to this disease.

AIDS is different from other life-threatening conditions, and so are the needs of those affected by it. Issues of blame, accountability, and identity cross into the traditional arenas of fear, hope, and wholeness. Illness is personal, but the politics of AIDS are parked by the bedside and its sufferers cannot afford the luxury of silence. Despite the Center for Disease Control's estimate that 1 of every 250 Americans now carries the virus, people who are HIV-positive continue to face wide-scale ignorance and stigma. The incubation period is of unknown duration. Haunted by what is now known about transmission, people affected by HIV feel guilt and rage about what might have been prevented. And the illness—unlike cancer, in which tales abound of the patients who beat the odds—has yet to prove anything other than fatal.

There are many books on illness and loss, but they don't address those issues. The circumstances of people with AIDS require a particular sort of validation, and I hope that *Thinking Positive* will help provide it. That's why it includes sections on Accountability and Identity and Prejudice. That's why a wide variety of AIDS activists and spokespeople are quoted.

Yet the forces that isolate the AIDS patient ultimately pale beside those that unite them with people in crisis everywhere. Marianne

Williamson says, "I don't think AIDS is different from any other human heartbreak." It is by drawing upon our common humanity that we are rescued, perhaps even ennobled. Quotations in this book have particular relevance for people affected by HIV, but endeavor to guide and inspire them by calling upon universal themes of suffering, growth, and renewal.

A.A.

Accountability

NO ONE IS GUILTY. A POPULAR CONTEMPORARY SAYING is, *"All AIDS victims are innocent."* Others mutter, *"People with AIDS deserve it."* Both statements are problematic, because both encourage the impulse to blame. And blame, whether directed outward or inward, has no role here. No one deserves to be ill, whether with bunions or leukemia, whether from unsafe sex or an inherited condition. Ultimately, we are accountable only to ourselves.

As Joan Borysenko says, *"Let us try to remember that the only definition of sin that makes any sense is this: any thought or deed that perpetuates our ignorance of our own intrinsic goodness. We are healed when we can grow from our suffering, when we can reframe it as an act of grace that leads us back to who we truly are."*

In those early years, the federal government viewed AIDS as a budget problem, local public health officials saw it as a political problem, gay leaders considered AIDS a public relations problem, and the news media regarded it as a homosexual problem that wouldn't interest anybody else. Consequently, few confronted AIDS for what it was, a profoundly threatening medical crisis.

—*Randy Shilts*

To adults, the idea that we can assume responsibility for our wellness often suggests that we must be causing our own illness. Our self-doubt says, "If I am responsible, then I am to blame." Of course no one chooses to be ill on purpose or in any conscious way.... There is a world of difference between the fixing of blame and the accepting of responsibility.

—*Patricia Norris*

Considering illness as a punishment is the oldest idea of what causes illness, and an idea opposed by all attention to the ill that deserves the noble name of medicine.

—*Susan Sontag*

Never doubt that a small group of thoughtful, committed citizens can change the world. Indeed, it's the only thing that ever has.

—*Margaret Mead*

In our control-oriented, guilt-ridden society, AIDS is a failure of the individual. You are an "innocent victim" only if you get the disease due to circumstances beyond your control. Even so, "innocent victims" often report feeling guilty, as if they did something wrong, and they are certainly tainted with the stigma of AIDS after they're diagnosed. As Susan Sontag and others have pointed out, we view disease as something we've allowed to happen to us: we've failed to stay well. . . . We are obsessed with the idea that what we do or don't do is the number one reason why we get sick or stay well. We are equally obsessed with the belief that if we get sick, there must be something we can do about it.

—*Sharon Mayes*

To accept some of the responsibility for the disease, to realize that one has participated, is actually a very positive step. If one has taken part in getting sick, one can also take part in getting well.

—*Bernie S. Siegel*

I remember when Scott and I first talked to one another about our positive test results, how thrown we were, wondering what to do, how to handle it. We'd each had a hard time of it because so many people *expected* us to have AIDS. . . . We were two sexual outlaws of the Seventies, the ones who were supposed to get sick, so we were told, so people acted toward us. Now we were both infected and had to fend off the judgments that we "deserved" this illness.

—*John Preston*

The worst sin towards our fellow creatures is not to hate them, but to be indifferent to them: that's the essence of inhumanity.

—*George Bernard Shaw*

Is there any difference between standing by and watching (that is, giving tacit consent) while someone is being lynched, and making no effort to save a person dying of AIDS? I submit that there is no difference. . . . Degree be damned. If, as a society, we tolerate or encourage murder on any level, for any reason, we are capable of genocide.

—*Jed A. Bryan*

Each generation must, out of relative obscurity, discover its mission, fulfill it, or betray it.

—*Franz Fanon*

Responsibility, the high price of self-ownership.

—*Eli Schliefer*

People are always blaming their circumstances for what they are. I don't believe in circumstances. The people who get on in this world are the people who get up and look for the circumstances they want, and, if they can't find them, make them.

—*George Bernard Shaw*

If only one could have two lives: the first in which to make one's mistakes, which seem as if they have to be made; and the second in which to profit by them.

—*D. H. Lawrence*

You can't talk of the dangers of snake poisoning and not mention snakes.

—*C. Everett Koop, about AIDS education*

Separate the virus from a sense of punishment. . . . The virus does not set out to "get" anyone. . . . Nor does anyone set out to get infected with the virus. . . . Feeling guilty means worrying about something you cannot change. . . . Guilt uses emotional energy that would be better used on the real problems of life. Balance guilt by understanding your own worth. Ask yourself, outside my worries, who am I? . . . In the process, guilt usually fades away.

—*John G. Bartlett and Ann K. Finkbeiner*

The breeze of divine grace is blowing upon us all. But one needs to set the sail to feel this grace.

—*Ramakrishna*

Nowadays most people die of a sort of creeping common sense, and discover when it is too late that the only things one never regrets are one's mistakes.

—*Oscar Wilde*

Getting the disease through a sexual practice is thought to be more willful, therefore deserves more blame. Addicts who get the illness by sharing contaminated needles are seen as committing (or completing) a kind of inadvertent suicide. . . .Those like hemophiliacs and blood-transmission recipients, who cannot by any stretch of the blaming faculty be considered responsible for their illness, may be as ruthlessly ostracized by frightened people, and potentially represent a greater threat because, unlike the already stigmatized, they are not as easy to identify.

—Susan Sontag

As long as we are lucky we attribute it to our smartness; our bad luck we give the gods credit for.

—Josh Billings

When a person has sex, they're not just having it with that partner, they're having it with everybody that partner has had it with for the past ten years.

—Otis Ray Bowen

I learned that true forgiveness includes total acceptance. And out of acceptance, wounds are healed and happiness is possible again.

—Catherine Marshall

I can only say that, while my own opinions as to ethics do not satisfy me, other people's satisfy me even less.

—Bertrand Russell

People think responsibility is hard to bear. It's not. I think that sometimes it is the absence of responsibility that is harder to bear. You have a great feeling of impotence.

—*Henry Kissinger*

Unless you're ashamed of yourself now and then, you're not honest.

—*William Faulkner*

A large amount of research on people who've suffered catastrophe has proven that those who feel they contributed to it (even if they did not) tend to get over the trauma more easily than those who feel totally helpless. . . . Such an attitude enables people to accept human evil and natural disaster without believing that life is devoid of beauty or meaning.

—*Bernie S. Siegel*

There is only one morality, as there is only one geometry.

—*Voltaire*

If we . . . believe that the state of our bodies reflects our self-worth, we are really doomed to suffering.

—*Joan Borysenko*

Silence = Death.

—*Slogan of AIDS activists*

In our healing process, we choose not to see ourselves as victims, and to take responsibility for our thoughts and feelings. In that process, we learn that there is no one to blame.

—*Gerald Jampolsky*

Action

THE PEOPLE WHO GET THROUGH TOUGH TIMES BEST are the ones who stay engaged. *Whatever the crisis—whether a transition or a trauma, whether it's coping with a divorce or with a natural disaster—we need to find jobs to do, roles to maintain, avenues to pursue. We need to get out there, even if the farthest we reach is for the telephone.*

As social animals, we can't afford not to be busy. Whether mental or physical, activity is crucial in fighting depression, in defining our identities, and in learning what is uniquely ours to contribute to the world. We don't have to run a marathon or start an advocacy group, but withdrawal is not an option. Because, in Peter Levi's words, "Hope in every sphere of life is a privilege that attaches to action. No action, no hope."

Do the hardest thing on earth for you. Act for yourself. Face the truth.

—*Katherine Mansfield*

All the beautiful sentiments in the world weigh less than a single lovely action.

—*James Russell Lowell*

I don't want to die. I assume you don't want to die. Can we fight together?

—*Larry Kramer*

Agitators are a set of interfering meddling people, who come down to some perfectly contented class of the community and sow the seeds of discontent among them. That is the reason why agitators are so absolutely necessary.

—*Oscar Wilde*

Put your heart, mind, intellect, and soul even to your smallest acts. This is the secret of success.

—*Swami Sivananda*

When asked "What can you do?" I've found the answer frequently can be found by rearranging the words into the answer: "Do what you can." . . . There is one thing we can all do, and that is to listen.

—*Ted Menten*

Begin now—not tomorrow, not next week, but today—to seize the moment and make this day count. Remember, yesterday is gone and tomorrow may never come. Today is all we have.

—*Ellen Kriedman*

Nothing will ever be attempted if all possible objections must first be overcome.

—*Samuel Johnson*

Every normal man must be tempted at times to spit on his hands, hoist the black flag, and begin slitting throats.

—*H. L. Mencken*

Each and every day of my life I must act as if I already have AIDS and am fighting for my life.

—*Larry Kramer (1985)*

One of the most tragic things I know about human nature is that all of us tend to put off living. We are all dreaming of some magical rose garden over the horizon—instead of enjoying the roses that are blooming outside our windows today.

—Dale Carnegie

The only thing necessary for the triumph of evil is for good men to do nothing.

—Edmund Burke

Pray for the dead, but fight like hell for the living.

—Mother Jones

One hour today is worth two tomorrow.

—Thomas Fuller

Be not afraid of going slowly, be afraid only of standing still.

—Chinese proverb

The most decisive actions of our lives . . . are most often unconsidered actions.

—André Gide

Do what you can.

—*Sydney Smith*

Yesterday is a canceled check; tomorrow is a promissory note; today is the only cash you have—so spend it wisely.

—*Kay Lyons*

This illness gave me permission to change.

—*Dean Rolston*

No man knows what he can do until he tries.

—*Publilius Syrus*

Life is short, and the time we waste in yawning never can be gained.

—*Stendhal*

You had better live your best and act your best and think your best today; for today is the sure preparation for tomorrow and all the other tomorrows that follow.

—*Harriet Martineau*

Carpe diem. [Seize the day.]

—Horace

What you want to be eventually, that you must be every day; and by and by the quality of your deeds will get down into your soul.

—Frank Craven

Growth accelerates in this intensified climate. With nothing left to lose, risk takes on new meaning. Changes that were daunting before an HIV diagnosis seem like nothing compared to the prospect of dying without having done them.

—Mark Matousek

The world is divided into people who do things and people who get the credit. Try, if you can, to belong to the first class. There's far less competition.

—Dwight Morrow

Go ahead with your life, your plans, your preparation, as fully as you can. Don't waste time by stopping before the interruptions have started.

—Richard L. Evans

When you must, you can.

—*Jewish proverb*

To accomplish great things, we must dream as well as act.

—*Anatole France*

If there is no wind, row.

—*Latin proverb*

It is not impossibilities which fill us with the deepest despair, but possibilities which we have failed to realize.

—*Robert Mallet*

We must not let this awful sense of unknowing that AIDS yet represents divide us. We might all—every one of us—be potential AIDS victims. More than ever before we must fight together now—to help those who are already ill with AIDS, and to help insure our own future on this earth.

—*Appeal from the board of the Gay Men's Health Crisis*

You must live in the present, launch yourself on every wave, find your eternity in each moment. Fools stand on their island opportunities and look toward another land. There is no other land; there is no other life but this, or the likes of this.

—*Henry David Thoreau*

Work while you have the light. You are responsible for the talent that has been entrusted to you.

—*Henri F. Amiel*

I do not believe in a fate that falls on men however they act; but I do believe in a fate that falls on them unless they act.

—*G. K. Chesterton*

Adversity

IT'S HARD TO FACE ANY ILLNESS WITH GRACE. FOR THE HIV-positive, there's so much more to cope with: the unknown prognosis, the friend who no longer picks leftovers off the plate, the death of people deeply loved and missed, the cheek turned away, orange bags in the hospital that scream: DANGER—AIDS, as though the contents were radioactive. There is also the exhausting need to protect anyone, especially a child with HIV, from scrutiny, isolation, and rejection. Coupled with the unspeakable burden of the diagnosis itself are, at best, countless hassles and insensitivities; at worst, bigotry and cruelty.

Few of us would choose such hardships, and certainly not for those we love. But adversity can summon up faculties that might otherwise remain un-

recognized and untested. In Rainer Maria Rilke's words, "In the difficult are the friendly forces, the hands that work on us." Adversity has a far greater power to transform us than the unchallenged life.

There is only one genuine misfortune: not to be born.

—*Joaquim Maria Machado de Assis*

Nothing is particularly hard if you divide it into small jobs.

—*Henry Ford*

It will be years and years before we understand the magnitude of this AIDS experience. I wonder that it may prove to be one of the major events of late-twentieth-century culture. The minstrels become Greek chorus.

—*Allan Troxler*

Laughter is the only thing that'll cut trouble down to a size where you can talk to it.

—*Dan Jenkins*

In the depth of winter, I finally learned that within me there lay an invincible summer.

—*Albert Camus*

People affected by HIV infection know that their emotions—depression, anger, fear, guilt, dependency—though painful to feel and difficult to admit, are also realistic and perhaps inevitable. They know that despite the comfort of their friends and relatives, they must resolve these painful emotions alone. Their resolutions, though varied, are at bottom the same: somehow or other, they learn to deal with the conditions of life. . . . What this means . . . [is that] they are in charge.

—*John G. Bartlett and Ann K. Finkbeiner*

Some problems are just too complicated for rational, logical solutions. They admit of insights, not answers.

—*Jerome Wiesner*

People who don't have nightmares don't have dreams.

—*Robert Paul Smith*

AIDS is not a condition to be managed, like high blood pressure or poverty. AIDS is not just a disease, like cancer or sickle-cell anemia. AIDS is not a chronic medical state, like diabetes—though it may become one. AIDS in our time is an *event*, a calamity, like a forest fire, like the blitz of London.

—*Michael Denneny*

You have to fight against illness as if you were Mike Tyson in the ring, pummeling and pouncing on it fast and hard.

—*Joseph Raymond*

It is only because of problems that we grow mentally and spiritually.

—*M. Scott Peck*

Deep, unspeakable suffering may well be called a baptism, a regeneration, the initiation into a new state.

—*George Eliot*

The Fear [of getting the disease] can be so wearing, so depressing, so constant that a friend who learned he had AIDS said, on hearing the diagnosis, "Well, it's a lot better than worrying about it."

—*Andrew Holleran*

I have yet to see any problem, however complicated, which, when you looked at it in the right way, did not become still more complicated.

—Poul Anderson

The greatest pleasure in life is doing what people say you cannot do.

—Walter Bagehot

There seems to be so much more winter than we need this year.

—Kathleen Norris

Too much happens. . . . Man performs, engenders, so much more than he can or should have to bear. That's how he finds that he can bear anything. . . . That's what's so terrible.

—William Faulkner

Even a happy life cannot be without a measure of darkness, and the word "happiness" would lose its meaning if it were not balanced by sadness.

—Carl Jung

These days my blood is an impressive and dangerous substance. It stands alone now, at attention in its test tube like a Messenger from *The Egyptian Book of the Dead.* It's hard to remain clear when a jackal-headed scientist weighs my heart against a white feather. In two weeks I will learn the results. . . . I hope I can get out of this alive, the mind says, referring to life and not *able* to imagine alternatives.

—*Robert Glück*

The man who is swimming against the stream knows the strength of it.

—*Woodrow Wilson*

Your pain is the breaking of the shell that encloses your understanding.

—*Khalil Gibran*

The ultimate measure of a man is not where he stands in moments of comfort, but where he stands at times of challenge and discovery.

—*Martin Luther King, Jr.*

Most of the things worth doing in the world had been declared impossible before they were done.

—*Louis Brandeis*

Man needs to suffer. When he does not have real griefs he creates them. Griefs purify and prepare him.

—*José Martí*

It is in the power of the soul to maintain its own serenity and tranquillity, and not to think that pain is an evil.

—*Marcus Aurelius*

Good people are good because they've come to wisdom through failure. We get very little wisdom from success, you know.

—*William Saroyan*

Where there is sorrow, there is holy ground.

—*Oscar Wilde*

The dark or sick days need not be seen as bad days, for they often prompt our deepest reflection and, in some cases, a change of life-style. In this sense, then, one can look upon darkness or disease not as an end but as a beginning of growth.

—*Eileen Rockefeller Groward*

Anger

ANGER IS BAD FOR YOUR BODY AND SPIRIT. IT IS NOT A solution, not an end in itself. But it is necessary, as a place many of us must pass through on our way to acceptance. Go ahead, rage. Rage at the death of someone you love and at the prospect of your own. Rage at the FDA and the insurance companies, at being turned away with some empty excuse by the dentist or haircutter you've patronized for years, at the PTA mom who wants an HIV-positive child to quit school, at the teenager who won't use condoms. Tell a friend who shies away from your embrace how that makes you feel. Admit that the demands of caregiving are relentless and grueling, and that there are times you deeply resent the sick person, even envy him.

Experience the catharsis. Then go beyond it.

Patients must be encouraged to express all their angers, resentments, hatreds, and fears. These emotions are signs that we care to the utmost when our lives are threatened.

—Bernie S. Siegel

Anybody can be angry—that is easy; but to be angry with the right person, and to the right degree, and for the right purpose, and in the right way—that is not within everybody's power and is not easy.

—Aristotle

If you are taking care of someone with the virus, understand that the disease is the target and you are not. The person you're caring for is feeling anger, not hatred; they do not blame you. . . . Still, you need not try to achieve sainthood during your lifetime. No caregiver is neutral . . . .

—John G. Bartlett and Ann K. Finkbeiner

The growth of wisdom may be gauged accurately by the decline of ill-temper.

—Friedrich Nietzsche

Oppression makes a wise man mad.

—Frederick Douglass

We are all crazy when we are angry.

—Philemon

It is unexpressed anger that is harmful. Too many people confuse anger with resentment. Anger can be positive, whereas festering resentment can cause people to become murderous. It is the things we have never said that harm us most.

—Bernie S. Siegel

Restlessness is discontent—and discontent is the first necessity of progress. Show me a thoroughly satisfied man and I will show you a failure.

—Thomas Alva Edison

We have petitioned and our petitions have been disregarded; we have entreated and our entreaties have been scorned. We beg no more, we petition no longer, we now defy.

—William Jennings Bryan

Unexpressed feelings depress your immune response.

—Bernie S. Siegel

If this article [reporting 1,112 confirmed cases of AIDS, in March 1983] doesn't scare the shit out of you, we're in real trouble. If this article doesn't rouse you to anger, fury, rage, and action, gay men may have no future on this earth. Our continued existence depends on how angry you can get.

—*Larry Kramer*

Never apologize for showing feeling. When you do so, you apologize for truth.

—*Benjamin Disraeli*

The strange things about healing . . . is that it often occurs with negative emotions as well. Negative emotions can be the trigger for someone to express honest thoughts in psychotherapy and in other healing modalities. In certain cases, negative emotions are essential to the healing process and are the only vehicle capable of taking the patient in a healing direction. For example, my friend Dr. Irving Yalom, who used to work with people with severe cases of cancer, found that all his patients died except one: a woman who got very angry at her disease. Her anger kept her alive.

—*Rollo May*

R̲esentment is like taking poison and hoping it'll kill someone else.

—*Alan Brandt*

N̲egative emotions will not harm you if you express them appropriately and then let them go. Bottling them up is far worse.

—*Joan Borysenko*

Attitude

IN A WORLD THAT OFTEN MAKES US FEEL POWERLESS, ONE *thing we can control is our attitude. Even in the most horrifying circum-stances, examples of the power of attitude exist: look at Anne Frank, or He-len Keller, or Nelson Mandela, or countless others who refused to accept pity or oblivion as their lot. No one can keep us down without our permission.*

We can envy others or we can take pleasure in what is ours. We can mourn those who have died, yet delight in the memory of their company. Bit-terness and self-pity tempt; but serenity, acceptance, happiness—even joy— are available to us as well. In choosing the latter course, we enlist an incredibly powerful ally: even the most traditional Western doctors now acknowledge that a patient's state of mind is the single most important factor in his or her recovery. A sense of well-being may require conscious effort, but it is ours to claim.

Obviously, positive attitudes are not a substitute for medical treatment but an integral part of it. One thing I have learned is that attitudes should not be underestimated in any assessment of the healing equation.

—*Norman Cousins*

Many AIDS patients, even more so than patients suffering from cancer or other life-threatening illnesses, are lacking in qualities of self-worth, self-esteem, and self-trust. These are blocked by a lot of guilt, shame, and ambivalence. Therefore, we first help them to get rid of their negativity. . . . Then, once they learn to love themselves and trust themselves, the spiritual dimension begins to open up. Only then are they ready for healing.

—*Elisabeth Kübler-Ross*

Confidence and hope do more good than physic.

—*Galen*

Studies of long-term survivors show that we take control of treatment and our lives. What does that mean? It means asking questions until you get answers that make sense. It means demanding accountability. It means evaluating what's important to you. And it means questioning authority every step of the way.

—*Robert A. Rimer and Michael A. Connolly*

Scientists who have studied responses to stress have found that ineffectual anger is the emotion most destructive to homeostasis. A serene acceptance of *what is* promotes health, but by keeping the mind clear it also puts a person in a better position to change things that need changing.

—*Bernie S. Siegel*

[The doctor] warned me to watch out for the depression that *often* accompanies a diagnosis of AIDS. So I said, with a great show of relief, "AIDS! Oh, doctor, thank God; I thought you said 'Age'!"

—*Robert Patrick*

It's okay to have AIDS. AIDS is not the end of the world.

—*Philly Lutaaya*

To be truly healthy and vitally alive, you need to do more than just eat right, exercise, and consult your physician. You also need something that transcends the physical. You need a healthy spirit—a health-promoting, life-affirming attitude.

—*Robert Rodale*

For peace of mind, resign as general manager of the universe.

—*Larry Eisenberg*

How am I? Well, when I think of what I've got, I feel like shit. But when I think of how I got it, I can't complain. How are you?

—*Robert Patrick*

Undisturbed calmness of mind is attained by cultivating friendships toward the happy, compassion for the unhappy, delight in the virtuous, and indifference toward the wicked.

—*Patanjali*

The reasonable man adapts himself to the world: the unreasonable one persists in trying to adapt the world to himself. Therefore, all progress depends on the unreasonable man.

—*George Bernard Shaw*

I was going to buy a copy of *The Power of Positive Thinking*, but then I thought : What the hell good would that do?

—*Ronnie Shakes*

Time has no divisions to mark its passage, there is never a thunderstorm or blare of trumpets to announce the beginning of a new month or year. Even when a new century begins, it is only we mortals who ring bells and fire off pistols.

—*Thomas Mann*

There is a useful and life-affirming kind of denial as well as the more usual self-destructive kind. In fact, I don't even call it denial. Rather, I call it bracketing: death is plainly marked and present, but suspended from consideration, so I can get on with living. The UCLA researchers, by the way, found this to be the most helpful strategy in coping with AIDS. They called it "the fighting spirit."

—*Jody Maier*

Worry is a thin stream of fear trickling through the mind. If encouraged, it cuts a channel into which all other thoughts are drained.

—*Arthur Somers Roche*

An interesting study, carried out at UCLA, involved fifty gay men with AIDS. The men who fared the worst were those who avoided thinking about AIDS altogether. They had the highest levels of concern about their health and about dying. They had the highest levels of depression and the lowest self-esteem. . . . Ignorance is not bliss, and denial is far from constructive—though there were certainly enough people who tried to convince me otherwise.

—*Jody Maier*

Your health is bound to be affected if, day by day, you say the opposite of what you feel, if you grovel before what you dislike, and rejoice at what brings you nothing but misfortune.

—*Boris Pasternak*

Sometimes it is more important to know what kind of patient has a disease than what kind of disease the patient has.

—*William Osler*

It is not what we see and touch or that which others do for us which makes us happy; it is that which we think and feel and do, first for the other fellow and then for ourselves.

—*Helen Keller*

God, give us the grace to accept with serenity the things that cannot be changed, courage to change the things which should be changed, and the wisdom to distinguish the one from the other.

—*Reinhold Niebuhr*

We are, perhaps, uniquely among the earth's creatures, the worrying animal. We worry away our lives, fearing the future, discontent with the present, unable to take in the idea of dying, unable to sit still.

—*Lewis Thomas*

Change has considerable psychological impact on the human mind. To the fearful it is threatening because it means that things may get worse. To the hopeful it is encouraging because things may get better. To the confident it is inspiring because the challenge exists to make things better. Obviously, then, one's character and frame of mind determine how readily he brings about change and how he reacts to change that is imposed on him.

—*King Whitney, Jr.*

Why not go out on a limb? Isn't that where the fruit is?

—*Frank Scully*

The world owes all its onward impulses to men ill at ease. The happy man inevitably confines himself within ancient limits.

—*Nathaniel Hawthorne*

I'm not advocating sexual promiscuity, drug use, suicide, or amorality. Rather, I'm advocating a critical analysis of our own barriers to understanding and compassion for the sick and dying, and a healthier respect for the objectivity, not the goodness or badness, of nature. I'm advocating the relinquishing of the idea that we, as individuals, can control the forces of nature.

—*Sharon Mayes*

Whoever is happy will make others happy too. He who has courage and faith will never perish in misery!

—*Anne Frank*

One's confidence, or lack of it, in the prospects of recovery from serious illness affects the chemistry of the body. The belief system converts hope, robust expectations, and the will to live into plus factors in any contest of forces involving disease. . . . Everything begins, therefore, with belief. What we believe is the most powerful option of all.

—*Norman Cousins*

Everything can be taken from a man but one thing: the last of the human freedoms—to choose one's attitude in any given set of circumstances, to choose one's own way.

—*Viktor E. Frankl*

The attitude of the healer is almost as important as the attitude of the person being healed.

—*O. Carl Simonton*

To wish to be healthy is a part of being healthy.

—*Seneca*

I'm not happy, I'm cheerful. There's a difference. A happy woman has no cares at all. A cheerful women has cares but has learned how to deal with them.

—*Beverly Sills*

A man's happiness or unhappiness depends as much on his temperament as on his destiny.

—*François de la Rochefoucauld*

Hungry Joe collected lists of fatal diseases and arranged them in alphabetical order so that he could put his finger without delay on any one he wanted to worry about.

—*Joseph Heller*

Of course there is no formula for success except, perhaps, an unconditional acceptance of life and what it brings.

—*Arthur Rubinstein*

Rule Number 1 is, don't sweat the small stuff. Rule Number 2 is, it's all small stuff. And if you can't fight and you can't flee, flow.

—*Robert S. Eliot*

It's true that tomorrow may be better—or worse. But today may not be so bad. You must appreciate the miracle that you're alive right now and forget about how, or if, you're going to live tomorrow.

—*Rod Steiger*

You are healed of a suffering only by experiencing it to the full.

—*Marcel Proust*

You can't turn back the clock. But you can wind it up again.

—*Bonnie Prudden*

I think we sometimes think only gay people can get it; it's not going to happen to me. And here I am saying that it can happen to anybody, even me, Magic Johnson.

—*Magic Johnson*

True contentment is a real, even an active virtue—not only affirmative but creative. It is the power of getting out of any situation all there is in it.

—*G. K. Chesterton*

Some people are always grumbling because roses have thorns; I am grateful that thorns have roses.

—*Alphonse Karr*

Reflect on your present blessings, of which every man has many, not on your past misfortunes, of which all men have some.

—*Charles Dickens*

To achieve great things, we must live as though we are never going to die.

—Vauvenargues

The real voyage of discovery consists not in seeking new landscapes but in having new eyes.

—Marcel Proust

However confused the scene of our life appears, however torn we may be who now face that scene, it can be faced, and we can go on to be whole.

—Muriel Rukeyser

Let us not bankrupt our todays by paying interest on the regrets of yesterday and by borrowing in advance the troubles of tomorrow.

—Ralph W. Stockman

In spite of illness, in spite even of the archenemy sorrow, one *can* remain alive long past the usual date of disintegration if one is unafraid of change, insatiable in intellectual curiosity, interested in big things, and happy in small ways.

—Edith Wharton

Saying good-bye can be a joy. As death approaches, we do not need to turn away in fear. Instead, we can choose to celebrate life and join hands with those we love. We can sing and dance and make merry in the face of the lengthening shadow.

—Ted Menten

Courage

DEALING WITH HIV TAKES IMMENSE COURAGE: THE courage to get tested; the courage to pick up the phone even though the news might be bad; the courage to talk honestly with a parent or child; the courage to love someone with AIDS; the courage to take on a new responsibility when just facing the day seems to require a superhuman strength. We need the courage to behave responsibly, the courage to learn about the disease and to stand fast. Each day is a test. Sometimes an hour can be a marathon.

The splendid thing about the human spirit is what the most "ordinary" person is capable of under extraordinary circumstances. You may think yourself inadequate, but if you are doing any of these things, you are brave enough.

We must face what we fear; that is the case of the core of the restoration of health.

—*Max Lerner*

Courage is not simply one of the virtues, but the form of every virtue at the testing point.

—*C. S. Lewis*

There comes a time in a man's life when to get where he has to go—if there are no doors and windows—he walks through a wall.

—*Bernard Malamud*

People affected by HIV infection face greater emotional strain than most people ever do. Furthermore, many face it at an unconscionably young age. There were many victims of the epidemic who fought rejection, fear, isolation, and their own deadly prognoses to make people understand and to make people care. Because of their efforts, the story of politics, people, and the AIDS epidemic is, ultimately, a tale of courage as well as cowardice, compassion as well as bigotry, inspiration as well as venality, and redemption as well as despair.

—*Randy Shilts*

God, give me guts.

—Eli Mygatt

Exceptional patients refuse to be victims. They educate themselves and become specialists in their own care. They question the doctor because they want to understand their treatment and participate in it. They demand dignity, personhood, and control, no matter what the course of the disease. It takes courage to be exceptional.

—Bernie S. Siegel

I believe that unarmed truth and unconditional love will have the final word in reality. This is why right, temporarily defeated, is stronger than evil triumphant.

—Martin Luther King, Jr.

The courage we desire and prize is not the courage to die decently, but to live manfully.

—Thomas Carlyle

To defend one's self against fear is simply to insure that one will, one day, be conquered by it; fears must be faced.

—James Baldwin

People with AIDS are the real heroes of our time, even more than those suffering from other diseases. Being young, many people with HIV embark on a kind of medical, psychological, and spiritual quest to find better treatments and discover themselves. It becomes a hero's journey.

—*Paul Bellman*

You gain strength, courage, and confidence by every experience in which you really stop to look fear in the face. You are able to say to yourself, "I lived through this horror, I can take the next thing that comes along." . . . You must do the thing you think you cannot do.

—*Eleanor Roosevelt*

The first and great commandment is, Don't let them scare you.

—*Elmer Davis*

Transcending fear opens the way to forgiveness of those who have wronged you, and it releases a love that can make you psychologically immune to your environment. Choosing to love and hold on to the meaning of life increases the chances of survival under *all* conditions.

—*Bernie S. Siegel*

Be strong and of a good courage; be not afraid, neither be thou dismayed: for the Lord thy God is with thee whithersoever thou goest.

—Joshua 1:9

Two o'clock in the morning courage: I mean unprepared courage.

—Napoleon

Oh courage . . . oh yes! If only one had that. . . . Then life might be livable, in spite of everything.

—Henrik Ibsen

For courage mounteth with occasion.

—Shakespeare

Cowardice, as distinguished from panic, is almost always simply a lack of ability to suspend the functioning of the imagination.

—Ernest Hemingway

Courage is resistance to fear, mastery of fear—not absence of fear.

—Mark Twain

A man does what he must—in spite of personal consequences, in spite of obstacles and dangers and pressures—and that is the basis of all human morality.

—John F. Kennedy

❧

Only the brave know how to forgive. . . . A coward never forgives; it is not in his nature.

—Laurence Sterne

❧

When the plague began and the television crews of certain stations refused to work on interviews with people with AIDS, I wanted to get their names, write them down, publish them on a list of cowards. When the parents in Queens picketed and refused to send their kids to school; when they kicked Ryan White out of class in Indiana; when people called in to ask if it was safe to ride the subway; when Pat Buchanan called for a quarantine of homosexuals; when they burned down the house in Arcadia, Florida, I felt a thrilling disgust, a contempt, an anger at the shrill, stupid, mean panic, the alacrity with which people are converted to lepers and the lepers cast out of the tribe, the fact that if Fear is contemptible, it is most contemptible in people who have no reason to fear.

—Andrew Holleran

❧

We also discovered that there is something more hideous, more atrocious than war or death; and that is to live in fear.

—*Eve Curie*

Bravery never goes out of fashion.

—*William Makepeace Thackeray*

Life does not give itself to one who tries to keep all its advantages at once. I have often thought morality may perhaps consist solely in the courage of making a choice.

—*Léon Blum*

It is a brave act of valor to contemn death; but where life is more terrible than death, it is then the truest valor to live.

—*Thomas Browne*

The only courage that matters is the kind that gets you from one moment to the next.

—*Mignon McLaughlin*

The eternal silence of these infinite spaces terrifies me.

—*Pascal*

When you don't feel yourself anything, I mean a part of anything, that's when you get scared.

—Lillian Hellman

Nothing is so much to be feared as fear.

—Henry David Thoreau

If you can keep your head when all about are losing theirs, it's just possible you haven't grasped the situation.

—Jean Kerr

A man can be destroyed but not defeated.

—Ernest Hemingway

Death and Dying

OUR SOCIETY PREFERS TO IGNORE THE REALITY OF death, but people dealing with AIDS have to look death in the face. AIDS has no cure yet. Most of its victims are young, so even the relative solace of a long life is denied. And while the hospice movement is gaining strength, helped by a growing number of health-care professionals, the medical establishment still tends to perceive death as a failure.

It is no failure, but a transition. Many New Age healers, in fact, feel that death can be an integral part of the healing process, and that healing may continue after the spirit has left the body. And while no one knows what comes next on the continuum, if we can move past our fear of getting there, peace of *mind is waiting. Someday we may all learn how to die consciously; people with AIDS are learning now.*

If we can learn to view death from a different perspective, to reintroduce it into our lives so that it comes not as a dreaded stranger but as an expected companion to our life, then we can also learn to live our lives with meaning—with full appreciation of our finiteness, of the limits on our time here.

—*Elisabeth Kübler-Ross*

I cannot forgive my friends for dying; I do not find these vanishing acts of theirs at all amusing.

—*Logan Pearsall Smith*

The heavens are too crowded with angels.

—*Tom Hanks, accepting an Oscar for his role in* Philadelphia

Do not go gentle into that good night.
Rage, rage against the dying of the light.

—*Dylan Thomas*

To live in hearts we leave behind is not to die.

—*Thomas Campbell*

I am always grieved when a man of real talent dies, for the world needs such men more than Heaven does.

—*Georg Christoph Lichtenberg*

Even the death of friends will inspire us as much as their lives. . . . Their memories will be encrusted over with sublime and pleasing thoughts, as monuments of other men are overgrown with moss, for our friends have no place in the graveyard.

—*Henry David Thoreau*

Even in terminal situations, healing can take place, even though it is not physical. Deep emotional and spiritual healing can accompany fatal illness as well as recovery, and we can learn to be a friend to that as well.

—*Martin Rossman*

When good men die, their goodness does not perish.

—*Euripides*

When you come to the edge of all the light you have, and must take a step into the darkness of the unknown, believe that one of two things will happen to you: either there will be something solid for you to stand on, or you will be taught how to fly.

—*Patrick Overton*

If you do not know how to die, don't worry. Nature herself will teach you in the proper time; she will discharge that work for you; don't trouble yourself.

—*Michel de Montaigne*

Death, be not proud, though some have called thee
Mighty and dreadful, for thou art not so,
For those whom thou think'st thou dost overthrow
Die not, poor Death, nor yet canst thou kill me.

—*John Donne*

Everybody has got to die, but I have always believed an exception would be made in my case. Now what?

—*William Saroyan*

Today I see that even death can be a form of healing. When patients whose bodies are tired and sore are at peace with themselves and their loved ones, they can choose death as their next treatment. They do not have pain because there is no conflict in their lives. They are at peace and comfortable. Often at that time they have a "little miracle" and go on living for a while, because there is so much peace that some healing does occur. But when they die they are *choosing* to leave their bodies because they can't use them for loving any more.

—*Bernie S. Siegel*

Acceptance of death is never easy. Perhaps if we could put our fear behind us and illuminate the passageway ahead, we would have an easier time. Still, those are not easy tasks. But once we have worked our way through anger, and denial, and avoidance, and bargaining, and promising, we come at last to that more peaceful space called acceptance. From that place we can more easily find our way to peacefulness.

—*Ted Menten*

I want to give it all away before some fool plays disco at my funeral and the record gets stuck and nobody can tell and the service goes on forever!

—*Robert Patrick*

That is happiness; to be dissolved into something complete and great.

—*Willa Cather (and inscribed on her gravestone)*

Death is not the greatest loss in life. The greatest loss is what dies inside us while we live.

—*Norman Cousins*

Thus that which is the most awful of evils, death, is nothing to us, since when we exist there is no death, and when there is death we do not exist.

—*Epicurus*

Death . . . is no more than passing from one room into another. But there's a difference for me, you know. Because in that other room I shall be able to see.

—*Helen Keller*

Most of us are uncomfortable in the face of death. Usually we try to put on a happy face and act perky. But that's not being truthful, and if there's one thing that someone facing death doesn't need, it's a lie.

—*Ted Menten*

Will AIDS patients ever reach a stage of acceptance and peace? Yes, the same is true as with all other terminally ill patients. If they receive and give themselves enough permission to express their anguish and their tears, their sense of impotence against a vicious killer virus and against a society that discriminates [and] blames . . . [and] if they have enough of a support system . . . then, and then only, will they develop the stage of peace and serenity that makes the transition we call death a quiet slipping over into another form of existence.

—*Elisabeth Kübler-Ross*

Death is nature's way of telling you to slow down.

—*Anonymous*

Some day the sun is going to shine down on me in some faraway place.

—*Mahalia Jackson*

It hath often been said that it is not death but dying which is terrible.

—*Henry Fielding*

I am prepared to meet my Maker. Whether my Maker is prepared for the ordeal of meeting me is another matter.

—*Winston Churchill*

Death is swallowed up in victory. O death, where is thy sting? O grave, where is thy victory?

—*1 Corinthians 15:54–55*

One world at a time.

—*Henry David Thoreau,*
a few days before his death

All interest in disease and death is only another expression of interest in life.

—*Thomas Mann*

Often we see people "heal into death" in such a way that those around the deathbed are left with a sense of greater completion and wholeness; and we know the real healing will continue even after death.

—*Stephen Levine*

Nothing seems so tragic to one who is old as the death of one who is young, and this alone proves that life is a good thing.

—*Zoë Atkins*

The only religious way to think of death is as part and parcel of life; to regard it, with the understanding and the emotions, as the inviolable condition of life.

—*Thomas Mann*

The general outlook is not that the person has died, but that the person has lived.

—*William Buchanan, on writing obituaries*

I want death to find me planting my cabbages.

—*Michel de Montaigne*

Healing may mean recognizing that it is okay to die. It may mean that the problems and conflicts posed to you for solution during this lifetime have been resolved and that you are now free to leave this environment.

—*John E. Upledger*

It's not that I'm afraid to die, I just don't want to be there when it happens.

—*Woody Allen*

✺

Usually death is one of the most individualizing and private experiences a person can undergo. But death is sometimes a social event, a shared reality; it was so in the trenches of World War I, in the gas chambers of Auschwitz, in the killing fields of Cambodia [and with the AIDS epidemic]. When death becomes a social event, the individual death is both robbed of its utter privacy and uniquely individual meaning and simultaneously amplified with the resonance of social significance and historical consequence. When death is a social event, both the individual *and the community* are threatened with irreparable loss.

—*Michael Denneny*

✺

To civilize death, to bring it home, and to make it no longer a source of dread, is one of the great challenges of the age. . . . Gradually, dying may come to hold again the place it used to occupy in the midst of life: not a terror, but a mystery so deep that man would no more wish to cheat himself of it than to cheat himself of life.

—The Economist

✺

Go away. I'm all right.

—*last words of H. G. Wells*

The subject no longer has to be mentioned by name. Someone is sick. Someone else is feeling better now. A friend has just gone back into the hospital. Another has died. The unspoken name, of course, is AIDS.

—*David W. Dunlap*

Quiet and sincere sympathy is often the most welcome and efficient consolation to the afflicted. Said a wise man to one in deep sorrow, "I did not come to comfort you; God only can do that; but I did come to say how deeply and tenderly I feel for you in your affliction."

—*Tryon Edwards*

The bitterest tears shed over graves are for words left unsaid and deeds left undone.

—*Harriet Beecher Stowe*

Healing is letting go of our fear of the concept of death, and recognizing that our true reality is a spiritual one—with no limitations. Healing means letting go of the concept that our identity is limited to a personality and a body that is doomed sooner or later to be hurt, to be rejected, get sick, and die.

—Gerald Jampolsky

Faith and Spirituality

FAITH IS THE ANTIDOTE TO FEAR, AND FEAR IS WHAT can paralyze the body and spirit. Doubt is faith's companion, and even those who seem to possess an enviably unwavering faith have usually arrived at it through ongoing struggle and questioning.

There are as many spiritual paths as there are beliefs. The way may be clear to us, or we may be closer to Ernest Hemingway's honest prayer: "Oh Lord, if there is a Lord, save my soul, if I have a soul." Wherever your spiritual route may lie, remember that seeking it is an end in itself. If the way is not clear, instead of blaming yourself, remember that you are part of an ongoing *process, a tiny piece in the puzzle of the universe and our quest for meaning. The only disservice to the self is not to search.*

Spirituality means the ability to find peace and happiness in an imperfect world, and to feel that one's own personality is imperfect but acceptable. From this peaceful state of mind come both creativity and the ability to love unselfishly, which go hand in hand. Acceptance, faith, forgiveness, peace, and love are the traits that define spirituality for me. These characteristics *always* appear in those who achieve unexpected healing of serious illness.

—*Bernie S. Siegel*

I've often said that HIV has actually changed my life, propelling me to change, encouraging me to confront what's difficult. . . . Like thousands of others living in this limbo, I've found depths and doors and potentials in extremis that I didn't know existed before. Forced to look beyond the body for metaphysical meaning, I've learned that within the horror lies a tremendous mystery.

—*Mark Matousek*

Kiss the flame and it is yours.

—*Thomas Lux*

The most beautiful thing we can experience is the mysterious. It is the source of all true art and science.

—*Albert Einstein*

I believe that man will not merely endure, he will prevail. . . . He is immortal, not because he alone among creatures has an inexhaustible voice, but because he has a soul, a spirit capable of compassion and sacrifice and endurance.

—*William Faulkner*

Prayer gives a man the opportunity of getting to know a gentleman he hardly ever meets. I do not mean his maker, but himself.

—*William Inge*

Although the bodily changes we call healings are not the automatic result of bringing the mind into accord with ultimate truth, they are the result of changing the mind. For example, if one *believes* that to experience the peace of God will change a particular physical state, then, quite naturally, this is the result. Belief, however, is not primarily conscious.

—*Hugh Prather*

The human body is an instrument for the production of art in the life of the human soul.

—Alfred North Whitehead

❦

Faith is much better than belief. Belief is when someone *else* does the thinking.

—R. Buckminster Fuller

❦

No faith is our own that we have not arduously won.

—Havelock Ellis

❦

The gay experience of AIDS as a call to spiritual consciousness and compassion is a step toward reclaiming the spiritual identity as shamans and witch doctors, faeries and oracles—mystical leaders—that gay historians and anthropological research reveal male and female homosexuals and cross-dressers have had in other cultures and other times.

—Toby Johnson

❦

Faith is the substance of things hoped for, the evidence of things not seen.

—Hebrews 11:1

❦

Until you know that life is interesting—and find it so—you haven't found your soul.

—Geoffrey Fisher

It is only by forgetting yourself that you draw nearer to God.

—Henry David Thoreau

Whether you are really right or not doesn't matter; it's the belief that counts.

—Robertson Davies

There is nothing more impressive than spontaneous prayer, because it involves long and arduous preparation.

—George Bernard Shaw

I would rather live in a world where my life is surrounded by mystery than live in a world so small that my mind could comprehend it.

—Harry Emerson Fosdick

The Lord is my strength and song, and he is become my salvation.

—*Exodus 15:2*

I would believe only in a God that knows how to dance.

—*Friedrich Nietzsche*

Often God has to shut a door in our face so that He can subsequently open the door through which He wants us to go.

—*Catherine Marshall*

The most beautiful thing we can experience is the mysterious. It is the source of all true art and science.

—*Albert Einstein*

I think it pisses God off if you walk by the color purple in a field somewhere and don't notice it.

—*Alice Walker*

Offer God anything to bring your brother back.
Know you have nothing God could possibly want.
Curse God but do not
abandon Him.

—*Michael Lassell*

The best prayers often have more groans than words.

—*John Bunyan*

We have only to believe. And the more threatening and irreducible reality appears, the more firmly and desperately must we believe. Then, little by little, we shall see the universal horror unbend, and then smile upon us, and then take us in its more than human arms.

—*Pierre Teilhard de Chardin*

For with God nothing shall be impossible.

—*Luke 1:37*

Health is the state about which medicine has nothing to say; sanctity is the state about which theology has nothing to say.

—*W. H. Auden*

Doctors don't know everything really. They understand matter, not spirit. And you and I live in the spirit.

—*William Saroyan*

The soul is dyed the color of its thoughts.

—*Marcus Aurelius*

He who does not believe that God wants this bit of sand to lie in this particular place does not believe at all.

—*Hasidic saying*

The true test of a man's worth is not his theology but his life.

—*The Talmud*

Affirmation of life is the spiritual act by which man ceases to live unreflectively and begins to devote himself to his life with reverence in order to raise it to its true value. To affirm life is to deepen, to make more inward, and to exalt the will-to-live.

—*Albert Schweitzer*

Faith and doubt are both needed—not as antagonists but working side by side—to take us around the unknown curve.

—*Lillian Smith*

We come. We go. And in between we try to understand.

—*Rod Steiger*

Well spake that soldier who being asked what he would do if he became too weak to cling to Christ, answered, "Then I will pray Him to cling to me."

—*Christina Rossetti*

The problem is not whether the song will continue, but whether a dark space can be found where the notes can resonate.

—*Rainer Maria Rilke*

Fear imprisons, faith liberates; fear paralyzes, faith empowers; fear disheartens, faith encourages; fear sickens, faith heals; fear makes useless, faith makes serviceable.

—*Harry Emerson Fosdick*

What is soul? It's like electricity—we don't really know what it is, but it's a force that can light a room.

—*Ray Charles*

But what is the difference between a real illusion and a healing religious experience? It is merely a difference in words. You can say, for instance, that life is a disease with a very bad prognosis, it lingers on for years to end with death; or that normality is a generally prevailing constitutional defect; or that man is an animal with a fatally overgrown brain. This kind of thinking is the prerogative of habitual grumblers with bad digestions. Nobody can know what the ultimate things are. We must, therefore, take them as we experience them. And if such experience helps to make your life healthier, more beautiful, more complete and more satisfactory to yourself and to those you love, you may safely say, "This was the grace of God."

—*Carl Jung*

Let the occasional spiritual flat tires redirect your life. That's what survivors do. They don't have failures. They have delays or redirections.

—*Bernie S. Siegel*

Prayer does not change God, but changes him who prays.

—*Søren Kierkegaard*

If a man will begin with certainties, he will end in doubts; but if he will be content to begin with doubts, he will end in certainties.

—*Francis Bacon*

The best way to know God is to love many things.

—*Vincent Van Gogh*

He who desires to see the living God face to face should not seek Him in the empty firmament of his mind, but in human love.

—*Fyodor Dostoevsky*

From the standpoint of a healer, I view spirituality as including the belief in some meaning or order in the universe. I view the force behind creation as a loving, intelligent energy. For some this is labeled God, for others it can be seen simply as a source of healing.

—*Bernie S. Siegel*

We must free ourselves to be filled by God. Even God cannot fill what is full.

—*Mother Teresa*

Here I stand; I can do no other. God help me. Amen.

—*Martin Luther*

The only effective answer to the problem of salvation must therefore reach out to embrace both extremes of a contradiction. Hence that answer must be supernatural.

—*Thomas Merton*

Humor is a prelude to faith, and laughter is the beginning of prayer.

—*Reinhold Niebuhr*

I am always humbled by the ingenuity of the Lord, who can make a red barn cast a blue shadow.

—*E. B. White*

Formerly, when religion was strong and science weak, men mistook magic for medicine; now, when science is strong and religion weak, men mistake medicine for magic.

—*Thomas Szasz*

Faith is the subtle chain which binds us to the infinite.

—*Elizabeth Oakes Smith*

The physical is the substratum of the spiritual; and this fact ought to give to the food we eat, and the air we breathe, a transcendent significance.

—*William Tyndale*

If we do discover a complete theory [of the origin of the universe], it should in time be understandable in broad principle by everyone, not just a few scientists. Then we shall all, philosophers, scientists, and just ordinary people, be able to take part in the discussion of the question of why it is that we and the universe exist. If we find the answer to that, it would be the ultimate triumph of human reason—for then we should know the mind of God.

—*Stephen Hawking*

Faith which does not doubt is dead faith.

—Miguel de Unamuno

The riddles of God are more satisfying than the solutions of man.

—William Hazlitt

How would man exist if God did not need him, and how would you exist? You need God in order to be, and God needs you—for that is the meaning of your life.

—Martin Buber

I believe in the forest, and in the meadow, and in the night in which the corn grows.

—Henry David Thoreau

In medicine, as in statecraft and propaganda, words are sometimes the most powerful drugs we can use.

—Sara Murray Jordan

What we are is God's gift to us. What we become is our gift to God.

—Louis Nizer

The religious vision, and its history of persistent expansion, is our one ground for optimism. Apart from it, human life is a flash of occasional enjoyments lighting up a mass of pain and misery, a bagatelle of transient experience.

—*Alfred North Whitehead*

How much more powerful is one fervent prayer than all the pride of man!

—*Hroswitha of Gandersheim*

All acts of healing are ultimately our selves healing our Self.

—*Ram Dass*

You can pray to the head of a sardine if you believe in it enough.

—*Japanese proverb*

The great act of faith is when man decides that he is not God.

—*Oliver Wendell Holmes, Jr.*

The great mystery is not that we should have been thrown down here at random between the profusion of matter and that of the stars; it is that from our very prison we should draw, from our own selves, images powerful enough to deny our nothingness.

—André Malraux

Friends and Family

WHEN TIMES ARE HARD WE DISCOVER FRIENDS WE didn't know we had, and it's surprising who becomes our true family. People we expect the most from often fail us, while others come through with astonishing steadfastness.

AIDS is a route for many into a system of love and support that would not otherwise have been revealed. AIDS is a catalyst for making peace with our families, mending fences, learning to love ourselves and those around us. Here is an opportunity to overcome the fear of being dependent or depended upon, and to grow together.

I don't believe that one person heals another. I believe that what we do is invite the other person into a healing relationship. We heal together.

—*Rachel Naomi Remen*

Balancing sympathy and intrusion is difficult. For people dealing with HIV infection, sympathy both as a blessing and a burden is as much a fact of life as the infection is.

—*John G. Bartlett and Ann K. Finkbeiner*

We are so fond of one another because our ailments are the same.

—*Jonathan Swift*

Everyone alters and is altered by everyone else. We are all the time taking in portions of one another or else reacting against them, and by these involuntary acquisitions and repulsions modifying our natures.

—*Gerald Brenan*

Each friend represents a world in us, a world possibly not born until they arrive, and it is only by this meeting that a new world is born.

—*Anaïs Nin*

A man finds his identity by identifying. A man's identity is not best thought of as the way in which he is separated from his fellows but the way in which he is united with them.

—*Robert Terwilliger*

True friendship is like sound health; the value of it is seldom known until it be lost.

—*Charles Caleb Colton*

Everything that irritates us about others can lead us to an understanding of ourselves.

—*Carl Jung*

I'm going to turn on the light and we will be two people in a room looking at each other and wondering why on earth we were afraid of the dark.

—*Gale Wilhelm*

Gratitude is the heart's memory.

—*French saying*

Be forgiving and be merciful, that is, be loving. Compassion is not enough—you have to demonstrate that you care. . . . Be respectful of difference. We are trying to help people with AIDS themselves, not make them over.

—*Jody Maier*

We do not quite forgive a giver. The hand that feeds us is in some danger of being bitten.

—*Ralph Waldo Emerson*

A friend is an absolutely phenomenal bit of good fortune in one's life.

—*Bob Ryan*

He that has lost a friend has more cause for joy that he once had him than of grief that he is taken away.

—*Seneca*

Friends are those rare people who ask how we are and then wait to hear the answer.

—*Ed Cunningham*

Do not believe that he who seeks to comfort you now lives untroubled among the simple and quiet words that sometimes do you good. His life has much difficulty and sadness and remains far behind yours. Were it otherwise he would never have been able to find these words.

—*Rainer Maria Rilke*

No act of kindness, however small, is ever wasted.

—*Aesop*

For people affected by HIV infection, the support of other people is as important to their minds as medication is to their bodies. . . . Supporters touch them, bring them things they like, and let them know they're valued. Supporters talk about themselves, and by doing that, give tacit permission to the person affected by HIV infection to talk as well. Supporters listen—without criticism, without advice, without too many suggestions for improvement, and with kindness.

—*John G. Bartlett and Ann K. Finkbeiner*

You will find, as you look back upon your life, that the moments that stand out are the moments when you have done things for others.

—*Henry Drummond*

The greatest object in the universe, says a certain philosopher, is a good man struggling with adversity, yet there is a still greater, which is the good man that comes to relieve it.

—*Oliver Goldsmith*

Because AIDS has brought gay men much closer so that friendships that would ordinarily take years to develop are now quickly made and cemented—those of us fighting this epidemic find ourselves with many new friends very quickly indeed. (It's not unusual to go to a funeral and find that most of the mourners are men and women the deceased became friendly with after his AIDS diagnosis.)

—*Larry Kramer*

A good listener is not only popular everywhere, but after a while he knows something.

—*Wilson Mizner*

It is one of the most beautiful compensations of this life that no man can sincerely try to help another without helping himself.

—*Ralph Waldo Emerson*

No man is the whole of himself. His friends are the rest of him.

—Good Life Almanac

Other things may change us, but we start and end with the family.

—*Anthony Brandt*

I want to tell them: Do you love your children? Bring them home! You won't catch it. Hug them and kiss them and tell them you love them. That's what they need. . . . Love them and let them know it.

—*John Politan's mother, quoted by E. J. Graff*

Friends are relatives you make for yourself.

—*Eustache Deschamps*

Two important things are to have a genuine interest in people and to be kind to them. Kindness, I've discovered, is everything in life.

—*Isaac Bashevis Singer*

No one is useless in this world who lightens the burden of it to anyone else.

—*Charles Dickens*

Being part of a friendly and supportive group of people is one of the most valuable of all health-building activities. People truly are regenerative for one another.

—*Robert Rodale*

Kinship is healing; we are physicians to each other.

—*Oliver Sacks*

Three . . . are my friends. [One] that loves me, [one] that hates me, [one] that is indifferent to me. Who loves me, teaches me tenderness. Who hates me, teaches me caution. Who is indifferent to me, teaches me self-reliance.

—*Ivan Panin*

Friends are God's apology for relatives.

—*Hugh Kingsmill*

Go often to the house of thy friend; for weeds soon choke up the unused path.

—*Scandinavian proverb*

We are actors who have over-rehearsed our lines. . . . Give sorrow occasion and let it go, or your heart will imprison you in constant February, a chain-link fence around frozen soil, where your dead will stack in towers past the point of grieving.

—*Allen Barnett*

A faithful friend is a strong defense: and he that hath found such an one hath found a treasure.

—*Ecclesiasticus 6:14*

Friends are the thermometer by which we may judge the temperature of our fortunes.

—*Marguerite, Countess of Blessington*

The meeting of two personalities is like the contact of two chemical substances: if there is any reaction, both are transformed.

—*Carl Jung*

Good friends are good for your health.

—*Irwin Sarason*

So long as we love we serve; so long as we are loved by others, I would almost say that we are indispensable; and no man is useless while he has a friend.

—*Robert Louis Stevenson*

The human heart dares not stay away too long from that which hurts it most. There is a return journey to anguish that few of us are released from making.

—*Ruth Pitter*

The deepest need of man, then, is the need to overcome his separateness, to leave the prison of his aloneness.

—*Erich Fromm*

[Illness] forces us to reach out for help, bringing more love to us.

—*O. Carl Simonton*

Constant attention by a good nurse may be just as important as a major operation by a surgeon.

—*Dag Hammarskjöld*

I put my hand where you lie so silently. I hope you will come glistening with life power, with it shining upon you as upon the feathers of birds. I hope you will be a warrior and fierce for change, so all can live.

—*Meridel Le Sueur*

If you and I are participating in the healing process together, it is my woundedness that allows me to connect to you in your woundedness. I know what suffering is. I also know that you may feel separated from other people by your suffering. You may feel lost, frightened, trapped. My woundedness allows me to find you and be with you in a way that is nonjudgmental. You are not the sick one or the weak one. We are here together, both capable of suffering, both capable of healing.

—*Rachel Naomi Remen*

You don't choose your family. They are God's gift to you, as you are to them.

—*Desmond Tutu*

Just as despair can come only to one from other human beings, hope, too, can be given to one only by other human beings.

—*Elie Wiesel*

I have been blessed with remarkable comrades and collaborators: together we organize the world for ourselves, or at least we organize our understanding of it; we reflect it, refract it, criticize it, grieve over its savagery, and help one another to discern, amidst the gathering dark, paths of resistance, pockets of peace and places from whence hope may be plausibly expected.

—*Tony Kushner*

Health and Healing

P EOPLE WITH AIDS HAVE AN EXTRAORDINARY MOTIVA-
tion to learn about the true nature of health and healing. Not only is this
a very powerful disease, it is a very new one. As we explore different
treatments and techniques, we come face to face with how complex the relationship between body and spirit really is. And the more we learn, the more
empowered we are. We may have AIDS, but healing is not out of our reach.

We need to take control of as much of our condition as we can, and to
learn when and where to let go. Accepting help can be the most generous step
of all, because healing works in two directions: in the process, our caregivers
too are healed.

∽ ∽ ∽

When the process of self-discovery has resulted in genuine self-healing, it may or may not produce a "cure"—that is, the elimination of symptoms. For true healing goes deeper than symptoms; it involves getting clear about your real identity and purpose in life.

—*John E. Upledger*

There are no such things as incurables, there are only things for which man has not found a cure.

—*Bernard Baruch*

The history of medicine reassures us that, with time and effort, the terrible mystery of AIDS will be unraveled and a cure found.

—*Kevin M. Cahill*

Our consciousness grows precisely because it cannot slough off the flesh. Consciousness is called to earth as humankind, mortal. All the great metaphysical truths become alive in the transforming paradox of living. There is an enormous challenge here that we seldom face. Yet every once in a while, one of us steps authentically into the midst of this great and mysterious drama and, at such moments, there is healing. And the greatest healing brings us more fully into life.

—*Richard Moss*

As long as a particular disease is treated as an evil, invincible predator, not just a disease, most people with cancer will indeed be demoralized by learning what disease they have. The solution is hardly to stop telling cancer patients the truth, but to rectify the conception of the disease, to de-mythicize it.

—*Susan Sontag*

We are now starting to collect the clues to the identity of the oldest and most reliable unseen ally of medicine. . . . The ally is the healer within each of us. And now, after centuries of being little more than a shadowy presence, a bit of medical folklore, it is beginning to reveal some of its secrets and its powers.

—*Steven Locke and Douglas Colligan*

Health is not a condition of matter but of mind.

—*Mary Baker Eddy*

The fact that the mind rules the body is, in spite of its neglect by biology and medicine, the most fundamental fact which we know about the process of life.

—*Franz Alexander*

The fantasy that a happy state of mind would fend off disease probably flourished for all infectious diseases, before the nature of infection was understood. Theories that diseases are caused by mental states and can be cured by will power are always an index of how much is not understood about the physical terrain of a disease.

—*Susan Sontag*

It is clear that as a society, we cannot longer afford a haphazard response to this public health crisis. We are beginning to recognize that the tragedy now striking gay men, Haitians, hemophiliacs, and drug users is, in fact, a national tragedy.

—*Theodore Weiss*

One of the basic principles of holistic health is that we cannot separate our physical body from our emotional, mental, and spiritual states of being. For instance, when we have a physical disorder, it is a message for us to look deeply into our emotional and intuitive feelings, our thoughts and attitudes, to discover how we need to take better care of ourselves emotionally, mentally, or spiritually, as well as physically. With this approach, we can restore the natural harmony and balance within our being.

—*Shakti Gawain*

It is not possible to heal the body without engaging the mind's support.

—*Meir Schneider*

Whether we are seeking to run from life to some illusion of security, or yielding ourselves into life's wonder . . . there comes a point when no effort consciously undertaken assures us of true healing. Our many triumphs must stand side by side with this deeper mystery in which we are humbled, even wounded in our pride.

—*Richard Moss*

All too often the victims of AIDS have been made to feel like Camus's victims, exiled and deprived of the full measure of what American medicine has to offer. But there have also been many instances of individual courage, of simple adherence by physicians and nurses and technicians to a code as old as medicine itself.

—*Kevin M. Cahill*

For me, the healing process is made up of unconditional love, forgiveness, and letting go of fear.

—*Gerald Jampolsky*

The successful therapeutic process does not necessarily produce comfort, ease, muscular strength, prolonged life, or any of the other things that our Western medical tradition has come to hold as evidence of healing. Effective therapy does, however, give the individual patient a clear vision of what he or she needs to do, as well as the strength and integration of mind, body, and spirit to do it. The goals of therapy are the elimination of delusion and self-pity and the helping of patients to prioritize and focus their lives so that they can grow.

—*John E. Upledger*

To heal the body without including the mind, without allowing the body/mind to sink into the heart, is to continue the grief of a lifetime.

—*Stephen Levine*

Genuine healing is a journey, facilitated by a healer, into a humanity deeper than the tragedy of any illness. The healer takes a person into the disorder and brokenness, whether it is curable or incurable, to find an intactness and reconciliation that profoundly reflects and manifests the genuine self.

—*Ted Kaptchuk*

The personality without conflict is immune from illness.

—*Edward Bach*

❧

The only way to keep your health is to eat what you don't want, drink what you don't like, and do what you'd rather not.

—*Mark Twain*

❧

I haven't been reading anything but condolence cards. A pixieish fellow P.W.A. sent one that says, "What do you give the man who has everything?"

—*Robert Patrick*

❧

In the West, where the meditative tradition is not strong and people are not in the habit of stopping periodically to become quiet and reevaluate their lives, illness stops a person so he can step back and have an opportunity to take stock of what is important to him.

—*Martin L. Rossman*

❧

The more serious the illness, the more important it is for you to fight back, mobilizing all your resources—spiritual, emotional, intellectual, physical.

—*Norman Cousins*

❧

I believe that all genuine healing addresses the problem of unblocking negatives in one way or another.

—*Sun Bear*

Bodily pain affects man as a whole down to the deepest layers of his moral being. It forces him to face again the fundamental questions of his fate, of his attitude toward God and fellow man, of his individual and collective responsibility and of the sense of his pilgrimage on earth.

—*Pope Pius XII*

Healing does not necessarily mean to become physically well or to be able to get up and walk around again. Rather, it means achieving a balance between the physical, emotional, intellectual, and spiritual dimensions.

—*Elisabeth Kübler-Ross*

Doctors pour drugs of which they know little, to cure diseases of which they know less, into human beings of whom they know nothing.

—*Voltaire*

Forty years ago the understanding of the immune system did not even amount to a pale outline of the detailed knowledge that is now accumulating at a phenomenal rate. . . . This is the fruit of a worldwide endeavor that recognizes no national boundaries.

—*Donald S. Frederickson*

Humor has much to do with pain; it exaggerates the anxieties and absurdities we feel, so that we gain distance, and, through laughter, relief.

—*Sara Davidson*

Grasping at healing, like grasping at enlightenment, results in unbearable suffering, for all grasping results in distress. But to allow ourselves to lighten, to allow ourselves to heal, to trust the process and enter into it without models or preconceptions of how we're supposed to be or who we're supposed to be, seems to be the very path that Healing and Light travel. When we remember that we are the path and that we must tread it ourselves—lightly, mercifully, and consciously—then the healing that goes beyond "healing" becomes our birthright, and we truly discover ourselves.

—*Stephen Levine*

There is nothing the body suffers that the soul may not profit by.

—*George Meredith*

I take the position that everything in the universe is trying to help us regain health and move in that direction. This is a very difficult concept for most of us to accept. . . . It can be done if we are open to it. The decision to be open is probably the most important single step toward healing. The concept of contacting the inner guide is one aspect of that decision. It means going inward, quieting ourselves, opening to help and asking for that help. This fosters the belief that help is available and strengthens the concept of trust.

—*O. Carl Simonton*

To me, healing is releasing from the past. . . . It is letting go of expectations, assumptions, and the desire to control or manipulate another person. . . . Healing is letting go of the fearful child so many of us carry inside, and awakening to the innocent child who has always been within us.

—*Gerald Jampolsky*

The present sufferers from AIDS are not on the fringes of society, but in the vanguard of civilization. The deadly force to which they have fallen may lie in wait for any of us or perhaps our succeeding generations. Patients whose disease we do not understand perform an essential service for mankind. They may give up their lives to point out areas of ignorance where common danger lies.

—*Donald S. Frederickson*

Many techniques and therapies are useful, but nothing is as effective as daily meditation practice to deepen the well from which the thirst for healing may be slaked.

—*Stephen Levine*

Any or all of the above-named ministrations [surgery, drugs, acupuncture, homeopathy, etc.] may be necessary to remove barriers to self-healing or to stimulate it, but they are not sufficient causes for healing. We know clinically and anecdotally that this is true. We know of patients who die despite "successful" surgery. Healing is a total, organismic, synergistic response that must emerge from within the individual if recovery and growth are to be accomplished.

—*Janet F. Quinn*

The extraordinary technology and powers of intervention that characterize modern medicine can eliminate many devastating symptoms in a flash; but they can also short-circuit a complicated system of suffering and meaning that is instrumental to life and consciousness. . . . We have developed so many tools, from visualizations to painkillers, for suppressing symptoms and their accompanying question marks that we have lost the ability to come to terms with pain and suffering, to be changed, informed, and even illumined by their presence in our lives.

—*Kat Duff*

When we are well, we all have good advice for those who are ill.

—*Terence*

Hope

TO BE HUMAN IS TO HOPE. IT'S ONE OF THE THINGS
*that sets us apart from the other animals, even when we're bone-tired,
beleaguered, fearful, sad. Hope is our most powerful, most ephemeral
weapon, not only in the struggle against illness and depression but in main-
taining the quality of a life worth living. Hope is what makes the difference.*

*Harvey Milk put it in perspective when he said, "I know that life can't be
lived on hope alone, but it can't be lived without it." Fortunately for us, it is an
unquenchable human impulse.*

HIV is the start of the next phase of your life. Don't lose hope, and don't give up. You're still a normal person, and you can still do a lot of the same things you did before.

—*Magic Johnson*

Hope is delicate suffering.

—*Imamu Amiri Baraka*

Charity is the power of defending that which we know to be indefensible. Hope is the power of being cheerful in circumstances which we know to be desperate.

—*G. K. Chesterton*

The essence of optimism is that it . . . enables a man to hold his head high, to claim the future for himself and not abandon it to his enemy.

—*Dietrich Bonhoeffer*

The human body experiences a powerful gravitational pull in the direction of hope. That is why the patient's hopes are the physician's secret weapon. They are the hidden ingredients in any prescription.

—*Norman Cousins*

Hope is the dream of a waking man.

—*Diogenes*

Notwithstanding the sight of all our miseries, which press upon us and take us by the throat, we have an instinct which we cannot repress and which lifts us up.

—*Pascal*

When fate knocks you flat on your back, remember she leaves you looking up.

—*Anonymous*

Necessity can set me helpless on my back, but she cannot keep me there; nor can four walls limit my vision.

—*Margaret Fairless Barber*

We live by our genius for hope; we survive by our talent for dispensing with it.

—*V. S. Pritchett*

Hope is the physician of each misery.

—*Irish proverb*

If we're happy, we're exploring. If we're unhappy, we're resisting.

—*Dean Black*

❧

We must accept finite disappointment, but we must never lose infinite hope.

—*Martin Luther King, Jr.*

❧

A year and a half ago, when the blood reports were no longer reassuring and showed the virus's silent work of ruin, I asked myself, "What's it going to be: the glass half-empty or the glass half-full?" Since I felt healthy, I decided to come down on the side of the living rather than focus on disease and decline.

—*Jody Maier*

❧

Everything that enlarges the sphere of human powers, that shows man he can do what he thought he could not do, is valuable.

—*Samuel Johnson*

❧

To believe a thing impossible is to make it so.

—*French proverb*

❧

An epidemic signifies an intensified struggle for adaptation between man and some other species of life. The history of such calamities adds up to a balance in favor of man. We have reason to be cautiously optimistic.

—*Donald S. Frederickson*

The most certain sign of wisdom is a continual cheerfulness; her state is like that of things in the regions of the moon, always clear and serene.

—*Michel de Montaigne*

The optimist proclaims that we live in the best of all possible worlds; and the pessimist fears this is true.

—*James Branch-Cabell*

Without humor there is no hope, and man could no more live without hope than he could without the earth underfoot.

—*William Saroyan*

The man who says it cannot be done should not interrupt the man doing it.

—*Chinese proverb*

Future doctors will clearly understand the mechanism of disease. They will know what goes wrong and be able to prevent, even reverse, the process.

—Lisa M. Krieger

Charity is the power of defending that which we know to be indefensible. Hope is the power of being cheerful in circumstances which we know to be desperate.

—G. K. Chesterton

The joyfulness of a man prolongeth his days.

—Ecclesiasticus 3:22

There is tremendous power in positive thinking. When you expect the best, you literally create a thought field that magnetizes that which you desire. Like attracts like.

—Douglas Bloch

Hope is the physician of each misery.

—Irish proverb

It will be possible to live with HIV infection and *not* be overwhelmed by it. It *is* possible to postpone becoming ill. And it *is* possible to live amidst this tragedy, to hold our heads high, to keep our eyes focused on the future. Though I can't know what the future may hold, I do know that for now, here, I am *well*, I am in control, and I have confidence.

—*Paul Reed*

In the long run the pessimist may be proved right, but the optimist has a better time on the trip.

—*Anonymous*

Cheerfulness, sir, is the principal ingredient in the composition of health.

—*Arthur Murphy*

Every heart that has beat strong and cheerfully has left a hopeful impulse behind it in the world, and bettered the tradition of mankind.

—*Robert Louis Stevenson*

Identity and Self-Reliance

WITHIN EACH OF US LIES EXTRAORDINARY STRENGTH and purpose, and AIDS calls on every ounce of it. In her book Illness as Metaphor, *written after she was diagnosed with cancer, Susan Sontag writes,* "Having cancer has been experienced by many as shameful, therefore something to conceal, and also unjust, a betrayal of one's body. 'Why me?' the cancer patient exclaims bitterly. With AIDS, the shame is linked to an imputation of guilt; and the scandal is not at all obscure. . . . It is not a mysterious affliction that seems to strike at random." *The result is that someone with cancer gets casseroles, hugs, and sympathy, while a person with AIDS may have to do without so much as a handshake.*

Such treatment makes life more difficult, but it does not define us. By the same token, membership in any "risk group" is irrelevant. Each of us is unique, each equally subject to the human condition. How we confront the epidemic is the ultimate expression of our identity. As we learn to rely on ourselves, each of us encounters previously unimagined inner resources. And none of us will be found lacking.

We share residence in a global village and membership in a global family. Although the family is divided by nation and race, gender and economy, once we are HIV-positive, the divisions fade. Suddenly, I am one with the child who walks the dusty roads of Nigeria, the grandmother who tends her infected family in Manila, the gay stockbroker in San Francisco, and every HIV-infected mother who longs to see her children grow to adulthood.

—Mary Fisher

If you can get back in tune with your body, it will tell you what it wants. One way of doing that is to start to have more faith and confidence in your own instincts, logic, and common sense.

—Harvey Diamond

Perhaps the grandest power of health is self-healing. I say "grandest" because it's the least expensive, most accessible, and, in some ways, the most potent of health forces. It's inexpensive because your body supplies it free. It's accessible because it's part of you. It's potent because through the immune defenses it can slay germs by the millions, repel countless ills, avert a hundred microscopic calamities.

—Robert Rodale

Nothing can bring you peace but yourself.

—Ralph Waldo Emerson

Experience is not what happens to a man. It is what a man does with what happens to him.

—Aldous Huxley

AIDS haunts us both asleep and awake, and it changes not just our behavior but our very conception of who we are and our belief in ourselves.

—Dennis Altman

The wise don't expect to find life worth living; they make it that way.

—Anonymous

In order to heal themselves, people must recognize, first, that they have an inner guidance deep within and, second, that they can trust it. . . . For the most part, we do not learn how to listen to ourselves. Consequently, we do not trust and take care of ourselves according to what our inner guidance is trying to tell us.

—*Shakti Gawain*

Psychoanalysis shows the human infant as the passive recipient of love, unable to bear hostility. Development is the learning to love actively and to bear rejection.

—*Karl Stern*

Nine tenths of modern science is in this respect the same: it is the product of men whom their contemporaries thought dreamers—who were laughed at for caring for what did not concern them—who, as the proverb went, "walked into a well from looking at the stars"—who were believed to be useless, if anyone could be such.

—*Walter Bagehot*

The world needs to know who dies from AIDS.

—*Larry Kramer*

Self-trust is the essence of heroism.

—*Ralph Waldo Emerson*

We do not receive wisdom, we must discover it for ourselves, after a journey through the wilderness which no one else can make for us, which no one can spare us, for our wisdom is the point of view from which we come at last to regard the world.

—*Marcel Proust*

For nowhere can a mind find a retreat more full of peace or more free from care than his own soul.

—*Marcus Aurelius*

I take all stories of miraculous healings, spontaneous remissions, and instantaneous cures as evidence for the remarkable self-healing abilities that are possible in all humanity.

—*Jerry Solfvin*

Every new adjustment is a crisis in self-esteem.

—*Eric Hoffer*

When this virus becomes a formal part of you, your identity shifts. In the same way that having a ring slipped on your finger serves to tie the knot, acknowledgment of HIV renders peaceful cohabitation with this strange bedfellow a necessary, everyday affair.

—Mark Matousek

What another would have done as well as you, do not do it. What another would have said as well as you, do not say it; what another would have written as well, do not write it. Be faithful to that which exists nowhere but in yourself—and thus make yourself indispensable.

—André Gide

When we really love and accept and approve of ourselves exactly as we are, then everything in life works.

—Louise L. Hay

We must use the inadequate metaphors available to construct a cultural space from which those people most affected in the epidemic, as well as those observing its radical ruptures from afar, can make sense of HIV and AIDS and make the necessary personal and social choices and resistances.

—Cindy Patton

When a person is depressed or confused, the physician's advice is just one part of the prescription for spiritual renewal. The patient needs to learn to look within to find his or her own strength. It's like dancing. You can't learn to dance by listening to someone explain it to you; you have to get up and do it.

—*Carl Hammerschlag*

How many cares one loses when one decides not to be something but to be someone.

—*Coco Chanel*

There is a logical progression that starts with self-awareness and ends with self-expression. But the term self-expression does not refer only to the ability to express oneself in words or even in deeds. Rather, it refers to every kind of activity or behavior, including "internal actions," such as thoughts and emotions, and also to one's physical health, which may be thought of as a kind of behavior (or expression) of the body. When one truly expresses one's essential self, health is a natural by-product.

—*Emmett E. Miller*

I don't have to be what you don't want me to be.

—*Muhammad Ali*

I live with AIDS. I'm a person *living* with AIDS, not an AIDS *victim* or an AIDS *sufferer*, and mercifully only from time to time an AIDS *patient*.

—Jody Maier

As a human being related to all living beings we must first be related to ourselves. We cannot understand, love, and welcome others without first knowing and loving ourselves.

—Jean Klein

Ultimately, we will be healthier, not because of new drugs or surgical techniques, but because of the things we will do for ourselves.

—Louis Sullivan

So fresh and exciting this walk up the road with haversack on my back. . . . Off all the wife, the mother, the lover, the teacher, and the violent artist takes over. I am alone. I belong to no one but myself. I mate with no one but the spirit. I own no land, have no kind, no friend or enemy. I have no road but this one.

—Sylvia Ashton-Warner

And then came now. Different times. . . . Now they know who we are. . . . We've found our voices. We know who we are. They know who we are. And they know that we care what they think. And all because of a disease. A virus. A virus that you don't get because you're Gay, just because you're human. We were Gay. Now we're human. . . . I love you more now that I did on our most carefree day. . . . And it's impossible. . . . We can never touch as before. We can never be as before. "Now" will always define us.

—*Harvey Fierstein*

You are as young as your faith, as old as your doubt; as young as your self-confidence, as old as your fear; as young as your hope, as old as your despair.

—*Samuel Ullman*

Of all the people you will know in a lifetime, you are the only one you will never leave nor lose. To the question of your life, you are the only answer. To the problems of your life, you are the only solution.

—*Jo Coudert*

If I'm ever to reach any understanding of myself and the things around me, I must learn to stand alone. That's why I can't stay here with you any longer.

—*Henrik Ibsen (Nora, in* A Doll's House*)*

Follow your own bent, no matter what people say.

—*Karl Marx*

In loving myself I gain the power of identity that is necessary before love for others is possible.

—*David G. Jones*

In proportion to the development of his individuality, each person becomes more valuable to himself, and is therefore capable of being more valuable to others.

—*John Stuart Mill*

It's supposed to be a professional secret, but I'll tell you anyway. We doctors do nothing. We only help and encourage the doctor within.

—*Albert Schweitzer*

What lies behind us and what lies before us are tiny matters compared to what lies within us.

—Ralph Waldo Emerson

While gay men have, so far, been those who have been most able to give witness to what has gone on, this disease is also striking hard at people of color, at women and their children. AIDS knows no ghettos, it has no sexual preference, and it has no morality.

—John Preston

The only freedom which deserves the name is that of pursuing our own good in our own way, so long as we do not attempt to deprive others of theirs, or impede their efforts to obtain it. Each is the proper guardian of his own health, whether bodily, or mental and spiritual.

—John Stuart Mill

No one can make you feel inferior without your consent.

—Eleanor Roosevelt

What matters is what you think about yourself. You must find the part in life that fits and then give up acting; your profession is being.

—Quentin Crisp

The turning point in the process of growing up is when you discover the core of strength within you that survives all hurt.

—Max Lerner

The role of the physician and other health care workers is to empower patients—to help them to take charge of their own lives.

—Clive Wood

The process of restructuring your life, of becoming an authentic person, means ceasing to think of yourself as a thing—a collection of habits, a job, a role. This is being a slave of your self-image, and in a sense, already dead. Instead, we try to help patients understand themselves as dynamic, ever-changing processes. This comes about by recognizing that we are all perfectly imperfect. We are all bound by the inevitability of death and the fact that certain choices may speed the destructive processes. Nor do we know exactly when we will die, and within that uncertainty we all have almost unlimited options.

—Bernie S. Siegel

Don't compromise yourself. You're all you've got.

—Janis Joplin

The capacity to be alone becomes linked with self-discovery and self-realization; with becoming aware of one's deepest needs, feelings, and impulses.

—*Anthony Storr*

Self-respect is the fruit of discipline: the sense of dignity grows with the ability to say no to oneself.

—*Abraham J. Heschel*

Character, like a photograph, develops in darkness.

—*Yousuf Karsh*

Enjoy your own life without comparing it with that of another.

—*Marquis de Condorcet*

HIV asks only one thing of those it attacks: Are you human? And this is the right question: Are you human? Because people with HIV have not entered some alien state of being. They are human. . . . Not evil, deserving of our judgment; not victims, longing for our pity. People. Ready for support and worthy of compassion.

—*Mary Fisher*

You do not need to leave your room. Remain sitting at your table and listen. Do not even listen, simply wait. Do not even wait, be quite still and solitary. The world will freely offer itself to you to be unmasked, it has no choice, it will roll in ecstasy at your feet.

—Franz Kafka

In solitude alone can be known true freedom.

—Michel de Montaigne

Get down to your real self . . . and let that speak. One's real self is always vital, and gives the impression of vitality.

—John Burroughs

People often say that this or that person has not yet found himself. But the self is not something that one finds. It is something that one creates.

—Thomas Szasz

Miracles don't come from the cold intellect. They come from finding your authentic self and following what you feel is your own true course in life.

—Bernie S. Siegel

The growth in self-awareness comes from becoming more and more who I am. It is less and less a struggle with myself. And it has less and less to do with anything I do. The only thing I do not have to struggle with is being myself.

—*John Bradshaw*

We must realize that sex is not the fabric holding our [gay] community together. . . . We must realize that we are much, much more, that we have a sense of self and identity and relating such as exists in any religion or philosophy or ethnic background, and in which sex plays no more a role than it does in heterosexual identity. And if it takes an emergency epidemic to teach us this lesson, then let this be one of life's ironies.

—*Larry Kramer*

First it is necessary to stand on your own two feet. But the minute a man finds himself in that position, the next thing he should do is reach out his arms.

—*Kristin Hunter*

Of all the traps and pitfalls in life, self-disesteem is the deadliest, and the hardest to overcome, for it is a pit designed and dug by our own hands, summed up in the phrase, "It's no use—I can't do it."

—Maxwell Maltz

In order to heal themselves, people must recognize, first, that they have an inner guidance deep within, and, second, that they can trust it. . . .When we begin to trust ourselves more, the body begins to renew itself and becomes healthy and filled with life energy.

—Shakti Gawain

When a cure is found and the last panel is sewed into place, the Quilt will be displayed in a permanent home as a national monument to the individual, irreplaceable people lost to AIDS—and the people who knew and loved them most.

—Cleve Jones, founder of the NAMES project

Life Itself

I N TONY KUSHNER'S PLAY ANGELS IN AMERICA, PRIOR
Walter, who is dying of AIDS, is offered a place in Heaven or the option of
returning to Earth to wrestle with his illness. "I choose life," he says.

We are gladdened, but not surprised. Because who among us does not
choose life, even the most curmudgeonly, even in the most desperate of circumstances? To the question of whether life is worth living, Samuel Butler re-
sponded curtly, "That is a question for an embryo, not for a man." And when
the emphasis is on the quality of life, not the quantity, the choice is not only human but revitalizing.

AIDS must be seen as this rent in the fabric of life, personal and public. Like other catastrophes, AIDS heightens our lives in a way that we would never want. I'm cast into the region of the uncanny, where animate and inanimate blur. I tell myself, I can't die this way, but of course I can. A sense of destiny asserts itself in the face of so many blighted ones—the "me" avid to continue being comes forward.

—*Robert Glück*

Finish every day and be done with it. You have done what you could. Some blunders and absurdities no doubt crept in; forget them as soon as you can. Tomorrow is a new day; begin it well and serenely and with too high a spirit to be cumbered with your old nonsense. This day is all that is good and fair. It is too dear, with its hopes and invitations, to waste a moment on the yesterdays.

—*Ralph Waldo Emerson*

By October 2, 1985, the morning Rock Hudson died . . . there were the first glimmers of awareness that the future would always contain this strange new word. AIDS would become part of American culture and indelibly change the course of our lives.

—*Randy Shilts*

That life is worth living is the most necessary of assumptions, and, were it not assumed, the most impossible of conclusions.

—George Santayana

Life means to have something definite to do—a mission to fulfill— and in the measure in which we avoid setting our life to something, we make it empty. Human life, by its very nature, has to be dedicated to something.

—José Ortega y Gasset

We are a spectacular, splendid manifestation of life. We have language. . . . We have affection. We have genes for usefulness, and usefulness is about as close to a "common goal" of nature as I can guess at. And, finally, and perhaps best of all, we have music.

—Lewis Thomas

If we had a keen vision of all that is ordinary in human life, it would be like hearing the grass grow or the squirrel's heart beat, and we should die of that roar which is the other side of silence.

—George Eliot

If art is to confront AIDS more honestly than the media has done, it must begin in tact, avoid humor, and end in anger. Begin in tact, I say, because we must not reduce individuals to their deaths; we must not fall into the trap of replacing the afterlife with the moment of dying. How someone dies says nothing about how he lived. And tact because we must not let the disease stand for other things. AIDS generates complex and harrowing reflections, but it is not caused by moral or intellectual choices. We are witnessing at long last the end of illness as metaphor and metonym.

—*Edmund White*

God did not make us to be eaten by anxiety, but to walk erect, free, unafraid in a world where there is work to do, truth to seek, love to give and win.

—*Joseph Fort Newton*

The beauty of the world has two edges, one of laughter, one of anguish, cutting the heart asunder.

—*Virginia Woolf*

I never allow myself to be bored, because boredom is aging. If you live in the past you grow old, and dull, and dusty. It's very nice, of course, to be young and beautiful; but there are other qualities, thank God.

—*Marie Tempest*

I have a new philosophy. I'm only going to dread one day at a time.

—*Charles M. Schulz*

In our description of nature the purpose is not to disclose the real essence of the phenomena, but only to track down, so far as it is possible, relations between the manifold aspects of our experience.

—*Niels Bohr*

There are only two or three human stories, and they go on repeating themselves as fiercely as if they had never happened before.

—*Willa Cather*

Millions long for immortality who do not know what to do with themselves on a rainy Sunday afternoon.

—*Susan Ertz*

We are experiencing a dawning recognition that while science constructs our reality, it cannot deliver on its promise to save us from our human limitations. This is especially evident in cultural and political responses to AIDS, which are at once a throwback to medieval notions of sin and disease, and a confrontation with a cybernetic future of new viruses and technologized sex.

—*Cindy Patton*

Life and time are our only real possessions.

—*Ray L. Wilbur*

May you live all the days of your life.

—*Jonathan Swift*

If you have a talent, use it in every which way possible. Don't hoard it. Don't dole it out like a miser. Spend it lavishly like a millionaire intent on going broke.

—*Brendan Francis*

I honestly believe that AIDS is a healing of our time. I believe it's where our teachers are being taught at this time and the teachers in love and in healing that are coming out of the AIDS epidemic will be some of the greatest teachers we've ever had.

—*Elisabeth Kübler-Ross*

Life is what happens to you while you're busy making other plans.

—*John Lennon*

To be concentrated means to live fully in the present, in the here and now, and not to think of the next thing to be done, while I am doing something right now.

—*Erich Fromm*

Life is subject to change without notice.

—*Richard Eaton*

Life is like a game of cards. The hand that is dealt you represents determinism. The way you play it is free will.

—*Jawaharlal Nehru*

Life's a tough proposition, and the first hundred years are the hardest.

—*Wilson Mizner*

Life's under no obligation to give us what we expect.

—*Margaret Mitchell*

Deal with your emotions and live as if you were going to die tomorrow. Later, if you still need to, you may have the time to look back and discover why you are who you are.

—*Bernie S. Siegel*

There is no meaning to life except the meaning man gives his life by the unfolding of his powers, by living productively.

—*Erich Fromm*

Let us endeavor to live so that when we come to die, even the undertaker will be sorry.

—*Mark Twain*

Most of the evils of life arise from man's inability to sit still in a room.

—*Pascal*

There are two great rules of life, the one general and the other particular. The first is that everyone can, in the end, get what he wants if he only tries. This is the general rule. The particular rule is that every individual is more or less an exception to the general rule.

—*Samuel Butler*

When I hear somebody sigh, "Life is hard," I am always tempted to ask, "Compared to what?"

—*Sydney J. Harris*

Dying is no accomplishment; we all do that. Living is the thing.

—*Red Smith*

All life is an experiment.

—*Oliver Wendell Holmes, Jr.*

Life does not cease to be funny when people die any more than it ceases to be serious when people laugh.

—*George Bernard Shaw*

We should be careful to get out of an experience only the wisdom that is in it—and stop there, lest we be like the cat that sits down on a hot stove lid. She will never sit down on a hot stove lid again—and that is well; but also she will never sit down on a cold one anymore.

—*Mark Twain*

Life is an offensive, directed against the repetitious mechanism of the Universe.

—*Alfred North Whitehead*

The art of life is to know how to enjoy a little and to endure very much.

—*William Hazlitt*

In the midst of all the doubts we have discussed for four thousand years in four thousand ways, the safest course is to do nothing against one's conscience. With this secret, we can enjoy life and have no fear from death.

—*Voltaire*

To live is to suffer; to survive is to find meaning in the suffering.

—*Viktor Frankl*

Life is easier than you'd think; all that is necessary is to accept the impossible, do without the indispensable, and bear the intolerable.

—*Kathleen Norris*

Life is like playing a violin solo in public and learning the instrument as one goes on.

—*Samuel Butler*

The measure of a man's life is the well spending of it, not the length.

—*Plutarch*

Life is a series of relapses and recoveries.

—*George Ade*

It has begun to occur to me that life is a stage I'm going through.

—*Ellen Goodman*

If you want my final opinion on the mystery of life and all that, I can give it to you in a nutshell. The universe is a safe to which there is a combination. But the combination is locked up in the safe.

—*Peter DeVries*

Grant me the strength, time, and opportunity always to correct what I have acquired, always to extend its domain, for knowledge is immense and the spirit of man can extend infinitely to enrich itself daily with new requirement.

—*Oath of Maimonides*

You are eternity's hostage, a captive of time.

—*Boris Pasternak*

Too often AIDS is shown as a sort of romanticized, one-hour, Camille-type affair. Anyone who's been close to someone who's been ill or died knows there's nothing romantic about it. . . . This is a calamity that often makes the rules of ordinary reality suspend and reality itself crack open. Whether the Angel [in *Angels in America*], for instance, is real, imagined, or hallucinated, is something I want the audience to wrestle with, as the characters do. There's no single answer.

—*Tony Kushner*

Always fall in with whatever you're asked to accept. Take whatever is given, and make it over your way. My aim in life has always been to hold my own with whatever's going. Not against; with.

—*Robert Frost*

Love

EMBRACING OURSELVES AND OUR FELLOW MAN IS A tall order at the best of times, and that much more difficult in the face of a fearsome epidemic. We tend to burrow in, to insulate ourselves from any troubles that don't directly concern us. AIDS offers us a momentous opportunity to call on our better selves: in Elisabeth Kübler-Ross's words, "We can make our choices based on love and begin to heal, to serve those with AIDS and other diseases, to show compassion and understanding, and finally, before it is too late, to learn the final lesson, the lesson of unconditional love."

The first step toward unconditional love is perhaps the hardest: to learn how to love ourselves. That's where healing begins and ends. John Lennon *wasn't quite right: Love isn't all you need. But self-love is the most important love of all.*

❧ ❧ ❧

Love is the most powerful healing force there is. Love stimulates the immune system. We cannot heal or become whole in an atmosphere of hatred. Love moves us from being a victim to becoming a winner.

—*Louise L. Hay*

Love is always respectful. Always. So keep that in mind when you hold the hand of someone you love when it's time to say goodbye. You may not share the same beliefs—God has a hundred names and a thousand faces—but no matter the name of the pilot, the destination remains the same.

—*Ted Menten*

Love is what you've been through with somebody.

—*James Thurber*

The sweet thing about his forgetting exactly who I am, during these awful bouts of dementia, is that he seems to fall in love with me again, fresh, each time I go to comfort him.

—*Stephen Greco*

It is this intangible thing, love, love in many forms, which enters into every therapeutic relationship. It is an element of which the physician may be the carrier, the vessel. And it is an element which binds and heals, which comforts and restores, which works what we have to call—for now—miracles.

—*Karl A. Menninger*

Love can't always do work. Sometimes it just has to look into the darkness.

—*Iris Murdoch*

I wrote [*The Normal Heart*] to make people cry. AIDS is the saddest thing I'll ever have to know. I also wrote it to be a love story, in honor of a man I loved who died. . . . I wanted people to see that gay men in love and gay men suffering and gay men dying are just like everyone else.

—*Larry Kramer*

If love is the answer, could you rephrase the question?

—*Lily Tomlin*

Someday, after mastering the winds, the waves, the tides and gravity, we shall harness for God the energies of love, and then, for a second time in the history of the world, man will have discovered fire.

—Pierre Teilhard de Chardin

Love consists in this, that two solitudes protect and touch and greet each other.

—Rainer Maria Rilke

We must learn to eroticize our wounds.
The new love means getting it up
for things that are falling apart.

—Charles Ortleb

I am convinced that unconditional love is the most powerful known stimulant of the immune system. If I told patients to raise their blood levels or immune globulins of killer T cells, no one would know how. But if I can teach them to love themselves and others fully, the same changes happen automatically. The truth is: love heals.

—Bernie S. Siegel

Love doesn't just sit there, like a stone; it has to be made, like bread; remade all the time, made new.

—Ursula K. Le Guin

Healing is accomplished through love and *is* love. And love is the uniting principle in all healing approaches.

—Hugh Prather

There is no surprise more magical than the surprise of being loved. It is God's finger on man's shoulder.

—Charles Morgan

In the final analysis, we must love in order not to fall ill.

—Sigmund Freud

Love in the therapeutic relationship is facilitated by the knowledge that we are mortal, that we are all going to die someday no matter how much we jog or love or eat organically grown vegetables. With this awareness I make the most of my life in the present moment, doing today what I would most like to do with the rest of my life.

—Bernie S. Seigel

Love received and love given comprise the best form of therapy.

—*Gordon W. Allport*

Remember that the loving response to AIDS is not about helping people with the disease to die poetically or enabling them to become martyrs or making them over into saints. The loving response is a way of empowering persons with AIDS so that they can do the best they possibly can, maximize their health, and cope with their problems at any time during their illness.

—*Jody Maier*

We like someone *because*. We love someone *although*.

—*Henri de Montherlant*

Finding the ability to love requires giving up the fear, anguish, and despair that many people nurture. Many people have a lifetime of unresolved angers circulating through their minds and causing new stress with each recall. Confronting them and letting go of them involves honestly facing your own part in the problem, and forgiving yourself as well as the others you've resented and feared. If you do not forgive, you become like your enemy.

—*Bernie S. Siegel*

Love is a medicine for the sickness of the world; a prescription often given and too rarely taken.

—*Karl A. Menninger*

If you wish to be loved, show more of your faults than your virtues.

—*Edward Bulwer-Lytton*

Love is letting go of fear.

—*Gerald Jampolsky*

There is no difficulty that enough love will not conquer; no disease that enough love will not heal; no door that enough love will not open. . . . It makes no difference how deeply seated may be the trouble; how hopeless the outlook; how muddled the tangle; how great the mistake. A sufficient realization of love will dissolve it all. If only you could love enough you would be the happiest and most powerful being in the world.

—*Emmet Fox*

All great problems call for great love.

—*Friedrich Nietzsche*

[And what can the caregiver do?] Help those of us who are troubled with AIDS to love ourselves, lesions and all. Helping us find that love within is the first step in empowering us to be as healthy as we can be.

—*Jody Maier*

The love we give away is the only love we keep.

—*Elbert Hubbard*

I believe that the common denominator of all healing methods is unconditional love—a love that respects the uniqueness of each individual client and empowers the client to take responsibility for his or her own well-being.

—*Jack Schwartz*

Love cures people, the ones who receive love and the ones who give it, too.

—*Karl A. Menninger*

I would rather have this volume [*Love Alone*] filed under AIDS than under Poetry, because if these words speak to anyone they are for those who are mad with loss, to let them know they are not alone.

—*Paul Monette*

Love is the only sane and satisfactory answer to the problem of human existence.

—*Erich Fromm*

We all have our own individual way of expressing love, and when we discover what it is, then we will live the longest, be the healthiest, and enjoy life the most, as well as become able to receive the most love from others.

—*Bernie S. Siegel*

Perseverance

KEEP IN TOUCH. REFUSE TO LET THE WORLD PASS YOU
by. Eat even if you're not hungry. Vote. Buy that flashy shirt. Start a
journal. Read the next quote. Walk around the block. Don't wallow in
self-pity. Don't give in to depression. Don't assume you deserve being scolded
like this, because who says you do?

The very uncertainty of a diagnosis of HIV is tremendously difficult to
live with. How long will I stay well? Will a cure be found? What will I have to
deal with? It gets really hard to establish goals and to stick with them. But it's
crucial. Because whether our goals are modest ("I'll do my exercises this morning") or extreme ("I'm going to look like Arnold Schwarzenegger by June"),

with effort and stick-to-it-iveness, some of them come true. And then we feel great, we live longer, we live better.

W hen you're dancing with a bear you have to make sure you don't get tired and sit down. You've got to wait till the bear is tired before you get a rest.

—*Dr. Joycelyn Elders, on working in public health*

I won't give up no matter what happens. I thank God for my unconquerable soul!

—*William Henley*

T oo many patients have refuted the melancholy predictions of physicians to warrant grim forecasts. . . . Although we ought never to underestimate the seriousness of a medical problem, it is equally important never to underestimate the ability of the patient to mount a prodigious response to the challenge of disease.

—*Norman Cousins*

A ll human wisdom is summed up in two words: wait and hope.

—*Alexandre Dumas*

I am not a perfect servant. I am a public servant doing my best against the odds. As I develop and serve be patient. God is not finished with me yet.

—*Jesse Jackson*

Never think that God's delays are God's denials. Hold on fast; hold out. Patience is genius.

—*Comte de Buffon*

[The challenge is seen] not as apocalypse now, nor as apocalypse from now on, but as getting the FDA and the NIH to expedite treatments, as working out manageable workloads with employers or thesis supervisors, as figuring out ways to cope with recurrent nausea, as figuring out ways to get down a *whole* peanut butter sandwich, as making time, not serving it.

—*Michael Lynch*

Continuous effort—not strength or intelligence—is the key to unlocking our potential.

—*Lianne Cordes*

Keep the faculty of effort alive in you by a little gratuitous exercise every day. That is, be systematically ascetic or heroic in little unnecessary points, do every day or two something for no other reason than that you would rather not do it, so that when the hour of dire needs draws nigh, it may find you not unnerved and untrained to stand the test.

—*William James*

To endure is greater than to dare; to tire out hostile fortune, to be daunted by no difficulty; to keep heart when all have lost it; to go through intrigue spotless; to forego even ambition when the end is gained—who can say this is not greatness?

—*William Makepeace Thackeray*

It is not always by plugging away at a difficulty and sticking to it that one overcomes it; often it is by working on the one next to it. Some things and some people have to be approached obliquely, at an angle.

—*André Gide*

It is for us to make the effort. The result is always in God's hands.

—*Gandhi*

I always remember an epitaph which is in the cemetery at Tombstone, Arizona. It says, 'Here lies Jack Williams. He done his damnedest.' I think that is the greatest epitaph a man can have—when he gives everything that is in him to the job he has before him.

—*Harry S. Truman*

God is a hard worker, but He likes to be helped.

—*Basque proverb*

When we do the best that we can, we never know what miracle is wrought in our life or in the life of another.

—*Helen Keller*

Nothing is impossible; there are ways that lead to everything, and if we had sufficient will we should always have sufficient means. It is often merely for an excuse that we say things are impossible.

—*François de la Rochefoucauld*

People do not lack strength; they lack will.

—*Victor Hugo*

Life was meant to be lived, and curiosity must be kept alive. One must never, for whatever reason, turn his back on life.

—*Eleanor Roosevelt*

Enjoy when you can, and endure when you must.

—*Goethe*

Fight one more round. When your feet are so tired you have to shuffle back to the center of the ring, fight one more round.

—*James J. Corbett*

Before you begin a thing, remind yourself that difficulties and delays quite impossible to foresee are ahead. If you could see them clearly, naturally you could do a great deal to get rid of them, but you can't. You can only see one thing clearly and that is your goal. Form a mental vision of that and cling to it through thick and thin.

—*Kathleen Norris*

Be patient with everyone, but above all with yourself.

—*St. Francis de Sales*

[U]lysses'] secret is that he endures. He accepts what the day brings. He may hunker down, but he never gives in. He takes life as it comes, and that is why he survives.

—*George Sheehan*

Never let your head hang down. Never give up and sit down and grieve. Find another way. And don't pray when it rains if you don't pray when the sun shines.

—*Leroy "Satchel" Paige*

Only through time time is conquered.

—*T. S. Eliot*

In his later years, Winston Churchill was asked to give the commencement address at Oxford University. Following his introduction, he rose, went to the podium, and said, "Never, never, never give up." Then he took his seat.

Endure and persist; this pain will turn to your good.

—*Ovid*

We must not, in trying to think about how we can make a big differ- ence, ignore the small daily differences we can make which, over time, add up to big differences that we often cannot foresee.

—*Marian Wright Edelman*

The best way out is always through.

—*Robert Frost*

Prejudice

T HE DICTIONARY DEFINES PREJUDICE AS "A. AN ADVERSE
judgment of opinion formed beforehand or without knowledge or exami-
nation of the facts. b. A preconceived preference or idea; bias." This, of
course, is exactly what HIV-positive people constantly face, in all sort of guises.
The panic and phobia of our society couples with the already terrible burden of
the diagnosis itself. The stigma is exhausting, demoralizing, frightening, enrag-
ing, unfair, and wholly unnecessary.

It is tempting to rant at the ignorant, to label them willfully ignorant, or
bigots, or worse. But while it feels good at the time, in judging who they are we
become what they are. If, instead, we can accept them as merely uninformed

(a curable condition, after all), and keep an open mind, we will be on our way to healing our society.

❧ ❧ ❧

Healing's opposite is judgment, and any system (or practitioner) of healing loses its effectiveness when it becomes judgmental. The pronouncement that cancer is caused by an inability to love or that colds are signs of lack of joy or that AIDS is a manifestation of sinful-mindedness would not be made in the first place if we had not already judged illness as wrong.

—*Hugh Prather*

Disease can be healed, if we are willing to change the way we think and believe and act.

—*Louise L. Hay*

We're all at risk. Everybody who has HIV or who has developed AIDS deserves our support and compassion. Let's put a stop to the hate and fear.

—*Magic Johnson*

Fear always springs from ignorance.

—*Ralph Waldo Emerson*

Disease has social as well as physical, chemical and biological causes.

—*Henry E. Siegrist*

It is important that people know what you stand for. It's equally important that they know what you won't stand for.

—*Mary Waldrop*

When AIDS first cast its deadly shadow across America, the nightmare was so new, so terrifying, that everyone drew back in shock and fear and ignorance. . . . Today the fear is slowly beginning to subside. Ignorance is giving way to enlightenment, and people are starting to act like human beings again.

—*Ted Menten*

In contrast to cancer, understood in a modern way as a disease incurred by (and revealing of) individuals, AIDS is understood in a premodern way, as a disease incurred by people both as individuals and as members of a "risk group"—that neutral-sounding, bureaucratic category which also revives the archaic idea of a tainted community that illness has judged.

—*Susan Sontag*

Books won't stay banned. They won't burn. Ideas won't go to jail. In the long run of history, the censor and the inquisitor have always lost. The only sure weapon against bad ideas is better ideas.

—*A. Whitney Griswold*

That which we understand, we can't blame.

—*Goethe*

Exactly what kind of socially constructed "cosmic" scheme can encompass AIDS? A divine punishment for the sexual revolution of the sixties? A strange eruption of chance once again in a world we like to think we're finally coming to grips with? Is this misfortune deserved? And are we once again driven to contemplate the fragile notion of a cosmic equity, a divine design hidden somewhere at the center of things? Interpretations can kill, and we'd better watch out who is making them.

—*Sam Coale*

I can stand what I know. It's what I don't know that frightens me.

—*Frances Newton*

A Ryan White still brings out the celebrities to publicly mourn the death of someone from AIDS. Never mind the many, many homosexual men who have made this world a better, brighter place by what they painted, or wrote, or designed, or interpreted or portrayed and who died from AIDS. We still feel safer saluting a child with a blood disorder than allying ourselves in any way with addiction or "abnormality." But the illness has forced some compassion on every community, even the most reluctant.

—*M. E. Kerr*

If you judge people, you have no time to love them.

—*Mother Teresa*

Any disease that is treated like a mystery and acutely enough feared will be felt to be morally, if not literally, contagious. . . . Contact with someone afflicted with a disease regarded as a mysterious malevolency inevitably feels like a trespass; worse, like the violation of a taboo.

—*Susan Sontag*

Our dignity is not what we do, but in what we understand.

—*George Santayana*

The moment we begin to fear the opinions of others and hesitate to tell the truth that is in us, and from motives of policy are silent when we should speak, the divine floods of light and life no longer flow into our souls.

—Elizabeth Cady Stanton

For all that AIDS has been a tragedy and a setback for civil rights–organizing efforts, it has also squarely established the existence and identity of a gay subculture, made "gay" a household word, and encouraged and legitimized intellectual investigation of alternative sexualities.

—Toby Johnson

The ignorant are always prejudiced and the prejudiced are always ignorant.

—Charles Victor Roman

Hate has no medicine.

—West African saying

If prejudice could reason, it would dispel itself.

—William Pickens

We have silly and arbitrary definitions of sickness because we judge sickness as undesirable and unnatural, even as an indication of inadequate spiritual effort. . . . Once [conditions] are changed to fit our current picture of health, we believe the need for healing stops. A *judgment*, therefore, dictates when healing efforts begin, the target at which they are directed, and when they have accomplished their goal. . . . When the body becomes the major concern of the mind, the mind cannot fulfill its potential. Healing, if it is to have any lasting effect, must serve the mind and not be a tool of judgment, comparison, and classification.

—*Hugh Prather*

He prided himself on being a man without prejudice, and this itself is a very great prejudice.

—*Anatole France*

There is a link between imagining disease and imagining foreignness. It lies perhaps in the very concept of wrong, which is archaically identical with the non-us, the alien. A polluting person is always wrong, as Mary Douglas has observed. The inverse if also true: a person judged to be wrong is regarded as, at least potentially, a source of pollution.

—*Susan Sontag*

We should . . . recognize that there is no *intrinsic* connection between HIV and gay men or their sexual behavior. In this respect the continued homosexualization of HIV disease in the face of all the worldwide evidence concerning the diversity of social groups already affected strongly implies that the notion of HIV as a "gay plague" in fact protects heterosexuals from facing up to something which they find even more frightening than AIDS—namely the diversity of sexual desire.

—*Simon Watney*

Irrational barriers and ancient prejudices fall quickly when the question of survival itself is at stake.

—*John F. Kennedy*

We have to talk about liberating minds as well as liberating society.

—*Angela Davis*

Many people with HIV feel isolated and alone. People know when they're being treated differently. Don't be afraid to reach out.

—*Magic Johnson*

Prejudice is the chains forged by ignorance to keep men apart.

—*Marguerite, Countess of Blessington*

It is never too late to give up our prejudices.

—*Henry David Thoreau*

Priorities

WHEN FACED WITH A DEVASTATION SUCH AS AIDS, we learn what's really important in life. We take a step back. We consider the big picture. Do we have a parent it's time to reconcile with? Is there someone who's really important to you who might not know it? Is there a letter you've always meant to write, a place you've always wanted to visit, a piece of music you've yet to hear performed? Is there a child whose lifestyle you've never agreed with, but who nevertheless has a piece of your heart? Is there someone who should hear the truth? Or who deserves an open ear and mind, even if it's been a long time coming? Have you learned to love yourself, warts and all?

Go for it. Accept. Forgive. Love. Ultimately, what else matters?

[Psychologist Al] Siebert found that survivors have a hierarchy of needs and that, unlike most people, they pursue *all* of them. Beginning with the most basic, these needs are: survival, safety, acceptance by others, self-esteem, and self-actualization. One of the main needs that distinguished survivors from others, however, went beyond self-actualization: a need for synergy. Siebert defines the need for synergy as the need to have things work out well for oneself *and* others.

—*Bernie S. Siegel*

Nothing is worth more than this day.

—*Goethe*

Those in the trenches have had to be their own leaders, and they have done a superb job in trying to arouse a sleeping nation to the mounting danger. But perhaps we need to rethink our national priorities. . . . AIDS is only one of those problems [confronting America], but its grim nature symbolizes the potential disintegration of our culture if we do not take definite steps toward restoring it to good health.

—*Judith Laurence Pastore*

The excursion is the same when you go looking for your sorrow as when you go looking for your joy.

—*Eudora Welty*

What this epidemic teaches us is to become honest again, to talk and listen to each other, to accept and love each other more, and, most important, to learn to get our priorities straight.... Parents who never told a child that he was loved make the most heartfelt confession at the side of a son dying with AIDS. "They grow by leaps and bounds," as someone told me who shared the same experiences with formerly very reserved and "straight" parents.... Yet the question remains: "Why do we need such a harsh teacher?"

—*Elisabeth Kübler-Ross*

We never understand how little we need in this world until we know the loss of it.

—*James M. Barrie*

Once you have been confronted with a life-and-death situation, trivia no longer matters. Your perspective grows and you live at a deeper level. There's no time for pettiness.

—*Margaretta (Happy) Rockefeller*

It is not so important to be serious as it is to be serious about the important things.

—*Robert M. Hutchins*

Living with HIV involves surprises and unexpected changes. You can't predict or manage everything. . . . You have to put the living back into "living with HIV." Being flexible is the first step. Reclaiming your sense of the future is the second.

—*Robert A. Rimer and Michael A. Connolly*

Thank heavens, the sun has gone in, and I don't have to go out and enjoy it.

—*Logan Pearsall Smith*

People who know they are going to die spend their remaining time either a) being alive; or b) staying alive. . . . For people with AIDS, the desire to stay alive is urgent as they scramble for treatments to delay their deaths, knowing that a cure may be years away. It's natural to want to survive. But often the frantic search for a wonder drug or a miracle cure only speeds the progress of the disease instead of retarding it. And all too often the process of staying alive destroys the process of being alive.

—*Ted Menten*

The art of being wise is the art of knowing what to overlook.

—*William James*

You're only here for a short visit. Don't hurry. Don't worry. And be sure to smell the flowers along the way.

—*Walter Hagen*

I have enough money to last me the rest of my life, unless I buy something.

—*Jackie Mason*

Is it possible that our AIDS patients, children and adults alike, chose to contribute their short life spans on planet Earth to help us open our eyes, to raise our consciousness, to open our hearts and minds, and to finally see the light?

—*Elisabeth Kübler-Ross*

Won't you come into my garden? I want my roses to see you.

—*Richard B. Sheridan*

As I grow older, I simplify both my science and my religion. Books mean less to me; prayers mean less; potions, pills and drugs mean less; but peace, friendship, love and a life of usefulness mean more, infinitely more.

—*Silas Hubbard*

It is only with the heart that one can see rightly; what is essential is invisible to the eye.

—*Antoine de St. Exupéry*

Man's many desires are like the small metal coins he carries about in his pocket. The more he has the more they weight him down.

—*Satya Sai Baba*

One must learn to be concentrated in everything one does, in listening to music, in reading a book, in talking to a person, in seeing a view. The activity at this very moment must be the only thing that matters, to which one is fully given.

—*Erich Fromm*

I long to accomplish a great and noble task, but it is my chief duty to accomplish small tasks as if they were great and noble.

—*Helen Keller*

You can't go very far if you don't begin very near.

—*J. Krishnamurti*

The only real satisfaction there is, is to be growing up inwardly all the time, becoming more just, true, generous, simple, manly, womanly, kind, active. And this can we all do, by doing each day the day's work as well as we can.

—*James Freeman Clark*

Besides the noble art of getting things done, there is the noble art of leaving things undone. The wisdom of all life consists in the elimination of nonessentials.

—*Lin Yutang*

Mental health professionals who deal with people affected by HIV infection agree that the best strategies are whatever works. Nevertheless [there are] a few general guidelines. The first is to protect your physical health. . . . The second is to cultivate emotional health. . . . The third guideline is to take control of your life. . . . Satisfy these and any other principles you hold yourself to. Then trust yourself and live the way you feel you must. People affected by HIV infection say the same thing this way: be kind to yourself and others, come to terms with yourself, love yourself, trust yourself.

—*John G. Bartlett and Ann K. Finkbeiner*

I came to understand that it was all right to do things for people as long as I did it for the sake of doing it . . . the value being more in the act than in the result.

—*Joanna Field*

An old man was walking on the beach at dawn when he came across a young man picking up starfish stranded on the sand and throwing them back into the ocean. They struck up a conversation, and the young man explained that the starfish would die when the morning sun caught them. "But the beach goes on for miles and there are thousands of starfish," the first man pointed out. "How can your efforts make any difference?"

The young man looked at the starfish in his hand, tossed it into the waves, and replied, "It makes a difference to that one."

—*Anonymous*

In the name of God, stop a moment, cease your work, look around you.

—*Leo Tolstoy*

A man is rich in proportion to the number of things which he can afford to let alone.

—*Henry David Thoreau*

Purpose

HUMAN BEINGS NEED A PURPOSE; IT'S PART OF OUR make-up. That's why we weave a complex set of obligations to family, friends, employers, organizations. These commitments lend our lives meaning; they define us; they give us a reason to get out of bed in the morning; and in so doing, they make our lives infinitely more worthwhile.

In the face of AIDS, it is especially important to seek out and maintain such connections. In fact there's nothing like a crisis to help us set our sights, prioritize, really focus. One person's goal may be to lobby Congress, educate the public, find a cure; another's may be to admire the sunrise each day. It doesn't matter. Purpose informs even the most circumscribed of lives, and dedication to it is a vital gift to ourselves and those who love us.

The human heart refuses to believe in a universe without a purpose.

—*Immanuel Kant*

Learn with me the lessons of history and of grace, so my children will not be afraid to say the word AIDS when I am gone. Then their children, and yours, may not need to whisper it at all.

—*Mary Fisher*

We can actually learn something from an illness that helps to bring us back into alignment with our potential for wellness. For we are always trying to maintain our alignment, balance, and growth in accordance with our purpose in life, whether we are fully conscious of that purpose or not. And there is a way of seeing and relating to symptoms that can actually help us to align the flow of energy in accordance with that purpose—a way that allows us to see illness as an opportunity.

—*Martin Rossman*

He who has a why to live can bear almost any how.

—*Friedrich Nietzsche*

Your heaviest artillery will be your will to live. Keep that big gun going.

—*Norman Cousins*

Man, unlike any other thing organic or inorganic in the universe, grows beyond his work, walks up the stairs of his concepts, emerges ahead of his accomplishments.

—John Steinbeck

Ɛ

I want to live and I want to love and I want, in the universal as well as the specific sense, all my brothers to try to understand why this epidemic is here—because I think there are reasons why it is here—and, with your understanding, to help us, for we, and I, desperately need help.

—Larry Kramer

Ɛ

Hold fast the time! Guard it, watch over it, every hour, every minute! Unguarded, it slips away, like a lizard, smooth, slippery, faithless, a pixy wife. Hold every moment sacred. Give each clarity and meaning, each the weight of thine awareness, each its true and due fulfillment.

—Thomas Mann

Ɛ

Never give in! Never give in! Never—in anything great or small, large or petty—never give in except to convictions of honor and good sense.

—Winston Churchill

Ɛ

Thousands of candles, carried by people with AIDS, are flickering in the night, asking the question of us, "When?" The answer to that question depends on the national will.

—*Mathilde Krim*

"I can't believe that!" said Alice.

"Can't you?" the queen said in a pitying tone. "Try again, draw a long breath, and shut your eyes."

Alice laughed. "There's no use trying," she said. "One can't believe impossible things."

"I daresay you haven't had much practice," said the queen. "When I was your age, I always did it for half an hour a day. Why, sometimes I've believed as many as six impossible things before breakfast."

—*Lewis Carroll*

To every thing there is a season, and a time to every purpose under the heaven.

—*Ecclesiastes 3:1*

The day is always his who worked in it with serenity and great aims.

—*Ralph Waldo Emerson*

In the past, by pressing against the impenetrable walls of AIDS issues that are out of reach—by trying to do it all—I squandered energy, increased stress and frustration, and lost time I could have used more happily. Instead, now I try to identify what's in my control and concentrate on those angles. In the absence of knowledge and effective treatments, both of which will come in time, I count on this strategy as my line of defense. It's what works for me.

—*Craig Rowland*

Look not mournfully into the Past. It comes not back again. Wisely improve the Present. It is thine. Go forth to meet the shadowy Future, without fear, and with a manly heart.

—*Henry Wadsworth Longfellow*

You can have anything you want if you want it desperately enough. You must want it with an inner exuberance that erupts through the skin and joins the energy that created the world.

—*Sheilah Graham*

There is nothing that has to be done—there is only someone to be.

—*Jacquelyn Small*

Just as there are no little people or unimportant lives, there is no insignificant work.

—*Elena Bonner*

The purpose of AIDS writing now is *to get it all down*. The purpose of the writer in the time of AIDS is *to bear witness*. . . . To live in a time of AIDS and to understand what is going on, *writing must be action. Writing must be accompanied by action. Writing is not what our teachers told us, something that stands alone.*

—*John Preston*

Blessed is he who has found his work; let him ask no other blessedness. He has a work, a life-purpose; he has found it, and will follow it.

—*Thomas Carlyle*

Whatosoever thy hand findeth to do, do it with thy might.

—*Ecclesiastes 9:10*

Any path is only a path, and there is no affront, to oneself or to others, in dropping it if that is what your heart tells you.

—*Carlos Castaneda*

The nobler, the higher, the greater our commitments, the more we become the person God intended us to be.

—*Elisabeth Kübler-Ross*

The tragedy of life doesn't lie in not reaching your goal. The tragedy lies in having no goal to reach.

—*Benjamin E. Mays*

There are several basic skills everyone with HIV needs. The first step is recognizing that life with HIV is ambiguous at best. After that, you'll find yourself much further ahead if you can: Set your own objectives; Gather information; Solve problems creatively; Negotiate; Pay attention to details; and Stay motivated. You don't need to excel at every task. When you have trouble, seek help. Get friends to do it with you. Or have them show you how.

—*Robert A. Rimer and Michael Connolly*

To have a grievance is to have a purpose in life.

—*Eric Hoffer*

When we are trying to decide what to do, or when we are not quite certain what we really want, we can usually find the answer just by tuning in to our inner wisdom. . . . Once we can contact that inner guide, we need only to ask ourselves, "What feels right to me? What do I really want? What is true for me at this moment? Where is my energy taking me right now?"

—*Shakti Gawain*

We succeed only as we identify in life, or in war, or in anything else, a single overriding objective, and make all other considerations bend to that one objective.

—*Dwight D. Eisenhower*

Resolve to be thyself and know that he who finds himself loses his misery.

—*Matthew Arnold*

Man is a stubborn seeker of meaning.

—*John Gardner*

The opposite of life is not death, it's indifference.

—*Elie Wiesel*

This is our purpose: to make as meaningful as possible this life that has been bestowed upon us; to live in such a way that we may be proud of ourselves; to act in such a way that some part of us lives on.

—*Oswald Spengler*

Wholeness

WE ARE ALL IN THIS TOGETHER.

Our health—and our life—is shaped by many elements which combine into an entity far more rich and complex than the sum of its parts. Holistic medicine deals with the whole system, believing it to have an independent reality which cannot be understood by addressing the isolated components. This means that the two-sided metaphor of illness as a battle, of viruses as "invaders" and T-cells as "lines of defense," mercifully becomes obsolete as we turn the combined energy of body and mind to healing our whole selves.

Like ripples on the surface of a pond, AIDS awareness is reaching into society at large. (Ironic, isn't it, how big the rock must be in order for people to *notice the splash?) Each of us, too, can be located at the center of a set of concentric circles: individual, family, culture, country, continent, ecosystem, planet, solar system, universe. Isolation, however desirable it may seem to some, is not an option. America has AIDS. The world has AIDS. We are all in this together.*

⊰ ⊰ ⊰

The funniest thing about it is that I've grown to love this way of life—the intensity, clarity, poignancy—the ability to see things at their value, to measure life, at last, by its true and terminal standard. I laugh louder these days and cry at nothing. I work until my fingers hurt and I exercise my heart in love. The future is a fantasy and I think almost nothing about the past. Of course, AIDS is terrible—a sentence to the guillotine. But terror can enlighten.

—Mark Matousek

Despise no new accident in our body, but ask opinion of it.

—Francis Bacon

The cure of many diseases is unknown to the physicians of Hellas, because they are ignorant of the whole, which ought to be studied also; for the part can never be well unless the whole is well.

—Plato

Rather than thinking of illness as disaster, we can think of it as a powerful and useful message. If we are suffering, it is a message that there is something to be looked at within our consciousness, something to be recognized, acknowledged, and healed.

—*Shakti Gawain*

Confronting AIDS as a monolith is humanly impossible, but individual to individual, the noises and news, whether bad or good, give us glimpses of ourselves. We are hardened by anger, misunderstanding, and fear, softened and lifted by love and courage that comes almost magically from out of nowhere. Our singularity and aloneness are shattered.

—*Larry Ebmeier*

I cannot but think that he who finds a certain proportion of pain and evil inseparably woven up in the life of the very worms will bear his own share with more courage and submission.

—*Thomas Henry Huxley*

The human body is like a bakery with a thousand windows. We are looking into only one window of the bakery when we are investigating one particular aspect of a disease.

—*Béla Schick*

It is best if doctors care more for the individual patient than for the special features of the disease.

—*William Osler*

Nothing worth doing is completed in our lifetime; therefore we must be saved by hope. Nothing true or beautiful or good makes complete sense in any immediate context of history; therefore we must be saved by faith. Nothing we do, however virtuous, can be accomplished alone; therefore we are saved by love.

—*Reinhold Niebuhr*

Body and souls cannot be separated for purposes of treatment, for they are one and indivisible. Sick minds must be healed as well as sick bodies.

—*C. Jeff Miller*

Health necessarily involves the coordination and congruence of all aspects of one's being, including communications and relationships with others and with the environment. It embraces every aspect of life, including diet, exercise, work, play, and relaxation.

—*Emmett E. Miller*

The best and safest thing is to keep a balance in your life, acknowledge the great powers around us and in us. If you can do that, and live that way, you are really a wise man.

—*Euripides*

Those who are living through AIDS are spinning an astonishing garment for the spirit, one that offers its gift not only to those stricken but to all who care to reach, to participate in the great life of the imagination and spirit that is human culture. Gay culture is a necessity for us and an offering to the rest. At the moment, the dominant culture mainly rejects the gift and spurns the giver, which is a great foolishness. The gift asks only to be taken, and in that sharing we begin to participate in the communities of all peoples. In that sharing we begin to learn how to live among a plurality of peoples and to move among a multiplicity of cultures, with whom we share the Earth even as they share with us the riches of their experiences and the wealth of their spirit.

—*Michael Denneny*

Close one sad eye. Yes. Close the other sad eye. Yes. I can see now.

—*Yehuda Amichai*

Ultimately we cannot separate the healing of the individual from the healing of the planet. . . . As we begin to heal ourselves as individuals, we also naturally shift the consciousness of the entire planet. And as the collective consciousness begins to shift, we are each in turn affected by it. Thus, the more people change their consciousness and their way of life, the more the world changes; and the more the world changes, the more individuals change.

—*Shakti Gawain*

Ask not that events should happen as you will, but let your will be that events should happen as they do, and you shall have peace.

—*Epictetus*

AIDS has to be mythologized and explained in ways that provide positive messages about Earth's ecology. AIDS, after all, is one of the first truly major ecodisasters of modern urbanity, and the gay community's collective response has been—at least in most instances—exemplary of the kinds of grassroots organizing and community mobilization for problem solving that will be demanded more and more in the future.

—*Toby Johnson*

Choose to love and make others happy, and your life will change, because you will find happiness and love in the process. The first step towards inner peace is to decide to give love, not receive it.

—*Bernie S. Siegel*

We must steadfastly practice peace, imagining our minds as a lake, ever to be kept calm, without waves, or even ripples, to disturb its tranquillity, and gradually develop this state of peace until no event of life, no circumstance, no other personality is able under any condition to ruffle the surface of that lake or raise within us any feelings of irritability, of depression or doubt . . . and though at first it may seem to be beyond our dreams, it is in reality, with patience and perseverance, within the reach of us all.

—*Edward Bach*

We must learn compassion for the world, not just for other human beings.

Metaphorically, AIDS manifests victimhood and defenselessness—that, indeed, is precisely what the virus causes. By responding with compassion, gay men and lesbians have demonstrated the proper cure for victimhood. As a world, we must learn compassion. And we must learn compassion for the world, not just for other human beings.

—*Toby Johnson*

We now understand our own health as something created through the pattern of our lives; and we are beginning to understand disease, not as something bad or evil that "comes to get us," but as a symptom of an imbalanced way in which we walk on Mother Earth. With this understanding we can begin the process of healing ourselves through proper nutrition, physical exercise, new beliefs, and a more healthy environment, as well as through the balancing of energies and the right use of medicines that stimulate the body's innate healing capacities.

—*Brooke Medicine Eagle*

Happiness is beneficial for the body, but it is grief that develops the powers of the mind.

—*Marcel Proust*

Three passions, simple but overwhelmingly strong, have governed my life: the longing for love, the search for knowledge, and unbearable pity for the suffering of mankind.

—*Bertrand Russell*

We may search for cures that focus solely on the individual person ad infinitum, even "mind cures." But no matter how sophisticated they may be, they will always prove insufficient, because the central problem—our belief that we are local, limited, individual creatures—will remain untouched. For this disease there is only one cure—the Great Cure, which comes about when we wake up to the nonlocal, unbounded nature of the Self.

—*Larry Dossey*